12 Miracles of
Spiritual Growth

12
Miracles
of Spiritual Growth

A PATH OF HEALING FROM

THE GOSPELS

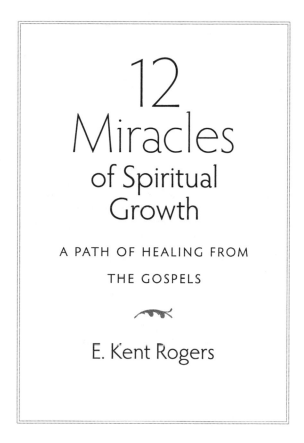

E. Kent Rogers

SWEDENBORG FOUNDATION PRESS West Chester, Pennsylvania

Library of Congress Cataloging-in-Publication Data
Rogers, E. Kent.
Twelve miracles of spiritual growth : a path of healing from the Gospels
/ E. Kent Rogers.
p. cm.
ISBN 978-0-87785-343-5 (alk. paper)
1. Jesus Christ—Miracles.
2. Bible. N.T. Gospels—Criticism, interpretation, etc.
3. Spiritual healing. I. Title.
BT366.3.R65 2012
232.9'55—dc23
2011044226

Edited by Morgan Beard
Design and typesetting by Kachergis Book Design

Printed in the United States of America

Swedenborg Foundation Press
320 North Church Street • West Chester, PA 19380
www.swedenborg.com

To Shovha, with whom I
gratefully share the road of
growing and healing.

Many thanks to Morgan Beard for her expert post-submission editing of this book and to Valerie Rogers for her pre-submission editing. I would also like to thank my parents, Ned and Val Rogers, for their early-stage editing, as well as my wife, Shovha, and children Alisha, Amrita, Avia, Chandra, Evan, Ganesh, Nick, Pasang, Puja, Rajendra, Santosh, Sharmila, and Sunita, for assistance with more recent editing of my life.

CONTENTS

INTRODUCTION

All the miracles the Lord himself performed when he was in the world symbolized the future state of the church. For instance, the eyes of the blind and ears of the deaf were opened, the tongues of the mute were loosened, the lame walked, and the maimed and leprous were healed. This meant that the kinds of people symbolized by the blind, deaf, mute, lame, maimed, and leprous would receive the Gospel and be healed spiritually, through the Lord's coming into the world. —EMANUEL SWEDENBORG, *SECRETS OF HEAVEN* §7337

I started writing this book after having looked deeply at a few of Jesus's healings. I found that the more I delved into these accounts, the more meaningful and personally therapeutic they became. I discovered that Jesus could heal me of spiritual problems today just as miraculously as he healed the physical problems of men and women two thousand years ago. Several times I felt the Lord reaching out through the text and through thousands of years, touching my heart and healing me. I saw that Jesus knows me, and all of us, in an intimate way. He knows about our fears, upsets, struggles, and hangups, and he answers us with the utmost compassion. I felt strongly that the healing I was receiving would be applicable and useful to others as well. I had to share what I had been given.

As the title implies, *Twelve Miracles of Spiritual Growth* explores the curative spiritual and psychological message contained in twelve of Jesus's healing miracles. I believe that this book is highly relevant to any Christian seeking a deeper, more meaningful relationship with Jesus. It will also appeal to the thoughtful spiritual seeker searching for spiritual solutions to psychological problems.

I have many non-Christian loved ones, and as this book drew near publication, I experienced some trepidation lest I alienate them by the boldness of faith I profess. So for them and for those other readers to whom faith in Jesus as the manifestation of Divine Love is a foreign or even off-putting idea, I wish to state the following. I believe in Jesus because I have found this belief to increase my desire and ability to love others. Faith is often criticized as divisive. I believe, not to separate myself from nonbelievers, but to be united with all people, regardless of faith, as my brothers and sisters. If there is anything of my faith that hinders my ability to have empathy with, relate to, or serve others, than I reject it as an erroneous aspect of faith.

I also feel a measure of foolishness in believing the antiscientific stories through which the life of Jesus is expressed—the virgin birth, the healing miracles, the resurrection, and even the idea that a man is God. Nevertheless, if belief in such stories is able to make me a better person—a more loving husband, a gentler father, a more trustworthy friend—then I am willing to subordinate logic and the desire for respectability to the goals of love. It is, in the end, exhilarating and liberating to have my life and, indeed, reality defined not by intellect, but by love. And ultimately, in my mind, that which increases love is the definition of logical. If something has a true and good effect in my life, then that thing, even if it appears fanciful, must be true and good. I've only ever found one thing as true and good as Jesus, and that is love itself; and for me, there is no difference between the two. Jesus explains to me how to love and Jesus inspires me to love beyond the borders of what I could otherwise have hoped for. Finally, Jesus grounds me. I marvel at people who love others well and simply without faith. I do not believe I am capable of this. Were I not able to point to Jesus as the source of love, I'd take credit and any love expressed would become adulterated with self-aggrandizement.

Who is Jesus, and what does faith in Jesus mean? Because this book is founded on stories about Jesus, these are important questions to answer. What is behind the words "I believe in Jesus"? To believe in something or someone, we must know their fundamental message and quality. Jesus twice expresses his message verbally: "This is my commandment, that you love one another as I have loved you. No one has greater love than this, to lay down one's life for one's friends" (John 15:12–13). He also states in the verses that follow that those who truly believe will live according to his commandments of love. In my mind, therefore, to believe in Jesus is to dedicate one's life to the effort of loving and serving others. Jesus didn't just preach this message, he lived it out in everything he did.

Heaven, Jesus says, is within. It is a spiritual state of mind. Love is the only source of lasting peace and true joy. I will use the word "love" frequently throughout this book, and since that word has so many diverging implications, it seems best to define the meaning I intend to communicate. Love is the essential nature of God, which we experience in several ways. When we are inspired by a heartfelt desire to bless others, to render them happy and improve their well-being, and when we feel genuine gratitude for the existence of others, that is one manifestation of Divine Love. I would equate this with the Holy Spirit; it is God's work and animation within us. So when I say that love is *the* heavenly state of mind, that is what I mean.

The activities that arise from that state of mind—the things we do from a heartfelt desire to improve life on earth and bless others—are a second manifestation of Divine Love. Only Divine Love can animate us to such selfless activity.

A third manifestation of Divine Love is Jesus—his life, his words, and his actions. God's love for the human race became incarnated as a Savior. Jesus is God and God is Love—all that Jesus ever said or did is the revelation of Divine Love. For this reason, I sometimes refer to God as Divine Love or simply Love. I do so when I mean to emphasize the immediate presence of God as love within human lives as opposed to intellectual knowledge and thought about God, which by nature distance us from the experience of God's immediate presence.

Love is what makes us truly human. In the absence of love, we are merely animals, biological machines. But love forms us into spiritual beings, transcending our self-serving, animal instincts. Love is more human than we are. Thus Divine Love, or God, is what is truly human and so authors our humanity. As our creator, Divine Love is not only human, but love is also divine. Were there no such thing as love, there could be no joy. Without joy there is no consciousness. Without consciousness, there is no reality. Thus Divine Love—who manifested as Jesus—is the source of all joy, all consciousness, and all reality. Because Divine Love is the source of consciousness, it is also the source of all intelligence. Therefore Divine Love is intelligence itself. Love is God, living and intelligent, both fully human and fully divine.

Love is heaven. Faith in Jesus delivers us into heaven because Jesus inspires selfless love, something that the self logically cannot achieve on its own. It is impossible for the self to transcend itself. Some repeat the idea that Jesus died for our sins. I believe that he died for our sins in the sense that he loves us even when our selfishness tries to block love from dwelling within us. In other words, our sins attempt to kill God's love, but Divine Love is willing to keep loving us anyway. And indeed that endless, steadfast mercy is our salvation. Faith is saving because it is the necessary bridge that allows us to aspire to a life in accordance with the will of Divine Love.

Since such intelligent, human Divine Love exists, it only makes sense that such a being would wish to contact us. Ironically, in the slow and halting development of my faith, the miracles of Jesus were previously uninteresting to me. I didn't want to base my faith on a belief in miracles. Rather, I first accepted Jesus as my personal God because of the value I found within his message. Nobody's message is so clearly true and good—*love one another*. He spoke the message I was willing to believe. I concur with what guards once said of him: "Never has anyone spoken like this" (John 7:46). Because I could believe in his message, I decided to believe in him. And so when he said, "Before Abraham was, I am" (John 8:58), I understood that the one who delivered this profound message was saying that he was also God.

That was many years ago. Since then, my faith has slowly but surely increased and filled out. What was at first a simple intellectual decision to believe in the man who spoke about love developed into an increasing trust of the heart. My ability to feel God's love and presence in life around me has steadily grown through the years. When God is felt all around, it is much easier to let go of fear and the selfishness it breeds. By relating to my Savior, I become a better person. He heals me and lifts me up. Since to transcend the self by means of the self is an impossibility, to be able to, little by little, transcend normal, natural, selfish instincts is the miracle of Jesus's love. While at first I found the written accounts of Jesus's miracles less meaningful, when parallel miracles began to occur in my own life, I was astounded and my faith was amplified. Jesus himself says, "Believe the works that you may know and understand that the Father is in me, and I am in the Father" (John 10:38). I see and appreciate the works that he brings forth in my life.

Apart from intensive study of the New and Old Testaments, the ideas in this book were also influenced by a number of other important factors. Understanding the Word of God as a parable or analogy of our personal spiritual development in our walk with the Lord is a concept thoroughly developed by the eighteenth-century mystic and theologian Emanuel Swedenborg, whose works I have read extensively. Similarly, other underlying theological ideas within this book, such as the singular personhood of God whose manifestation is Jesus and the inseparable nature of faith and love, are themes that Swedenborg discusses.

The value of working with others in groups for spiritual and psychological purposes is something I have experienced firsthand in a variety of contexts. I have had the privilege to gain the wisdom and blessing of all manner of individuals through Christian Bible studies, prayer groups, recovery groups, spiritual growth groups, and psycho-spiritual camp group encounters for many years. There is no doubt that these positive and sometimes life-changing experiences profoundly influenced the format of the practice espoused within this book. Though I wrote this book before my education in mental health counseling, I have since edited in a few ideas gained from that experience.

This book assembled itself piecemeal, chapter by chapter, as I came to see a message within each healing miracle. I chose the healings to meditate and write about randomly, without any particular order in mind. After reading each healing account, I would spend time in prayer and meditation. I also used Bible dictionaries and other reference books to learn more about customs, historical details, and the uses of various items mentioned. I used *Strong's Concordance* to learn the meaning of names and words. Sometimes the personal, spiritual message of the healing came quickly, sometimes slowly.

I chose to write about those healings that included the most amount of information. Sometimes the Gospels tell us that "all who touched him were healed." This is good news, but it lacks detail and so does not lend itself to in-depth exploration. However, other accounts of Jesus's healings provide rich detail and so paint a picture into which we can enter with our imaginations. These stories are like portals through which we can meet the living God. When I had exhausted the accounts that I felt called to write about, it turned out that I had twelve healings.

After completing the rough draft of each miracle, I wondered about the best order for the chapters. Initially, I considered dividing the miracles into categories, but I found that they didn't lend themselves neatly to such divisions. I was startled to discover that by ordering them in sequence as they occur in the text of the New Testament, they formed a continuous progression of meaning and healing—each story building upon the previous. The progression culminates in the raising of Lazarus (John 11), which on a personal, spiritual level also drew upon and bound together all the messages of the previous healing accounts. I had sometimes wondered why such an important miracle as the raising of Lazarus was not recorded in all four of the Gospels. Perhaps the answer is that the four Gospels taken together spell out the story of our spiritual evolution in a continuous manner. That special miracle in our lives, represented by the resurrection of Lazarus, only comes after we have traveled through the many other stages of our journey.

Each healing deals with a problem we face in our walk with Jesus. The healings deal with the problems in the order that we encounter them. It doesn't make sense to fine-tune our faith when we don't have any faith in the first place. Ordering the chapters according to the sequence in which they occur in the Bible made more sense and provided more progressive continuity from one to the next than any order I was able to devise on my own.

Of course, many of these stories can be found in more than one Gospel. In choosing which account to use, I first read each Gospel's version of the healing and then chose the one that seemed fullest with detail. In one case, the story of Malchus's ear, I included the account from all four Gospels, because each one adds an important piece of the story.

This is the order in which they occur both in the New Testament and in this book.

1. Canaanite's Daughter / Matthew 15:21–28 / Healing from feelings of unworthiness
2. Paralytic / Mark 2:1–12 / Healing from unforgiveness
3. Legion / Mark 5:1–20 / Liberation from addiction
4. Flow of Blood / Mark 5:21–43 / Release from inner warfare
5. Jairus's Daughter / Mark 5:35–43 / Restoration of innocence
6. Man's Son with Epilepsy / Mark 9:14–29 / Healing from doubt
7. Centurion's Servant / Luke 7:1–10 / Healing from faith-arrogance
8. Ten Lepers / Luke 17:11–19 / Healing from lack of joy

9. Malchus's Ear / Matthew 26:51–54; Mark 14:46–52; Luke 22:49–51; John 18:10–11 / Healing from fear

10. Man by Bethesda / John 5:1–14 / Healing from spiritual apathy

11. Blind Man / John 9:1–41 / Healing from blame-blindness

12. Lazarus / John 11:1–44 / Resurrection from spiritual death into spiritual life

Each chapter ends with suggested exercises. At least one of these exercises will be a meditation. Meditation is not as strange or intimidating as many imagine. In conjunction with my reading of the Word, I have found meditation to be perhaps the most profound agent in advancing the depth and meaning of my relationship with the Lord and thus also my relationship with others. Meditation simply means that you first relax body and mind and then focus exclusively on a certain mental activity. In these cases, the mental activity is to live through the miracles with as much imaginative detail as possible. The appendix at the end of this book explains a few ways to enter into a meditative state of mind from which one can embark on the specific meditations suggested at the end of each chapter.

Apart from the meditations, will be a list of "leaves," "fruit," and group discussion questions. The book of Revelation talks of the Tree of Life whose leaves heal the nations and whose fruit feed us. Just as leaves catch the light of the sun, so our thoughts are able to catch the light of God's ideas. And just as a tree uses the energy of light to grow, so we can use true ideas from God to grow strong and healthy. At the end of each chapter, under the heading "leaves," are a list of spiritual ideas contained in the healing of that chapter, which will heal us and cause us to grow.

At the end of each chapter, under the heading "fruit," is a list of actions we are encouraged to take, based on the lessons from that particular healing. When Jesus walked the earth, he said, "My food is to do the will of God." So, too, we are spiritually fed when we train our actions onto God's will, which is to say, the actions of love. Just as the body craves food and is made contented when food is eaten, so our spirit is only filled when we take loving and healing action. Deep inside our spirits, we all long to feel united to others and to know that our lives have a point. There is nothing that can satisfy that need other than love-based activities. Doing God's will truly is the fruit, the food, that feeds our spirit.

One of the underlying tenets of the book is that our spiritual wounds and weaknesses are actually blessings in disguise. The Lord of Love uses our weaknesses as an important arena to reveal himself. For each of our weaknesses, he has strength. For each of our spiritual illnesses, he has the cure. For a hardened heart, he has mercy.

Our liabilities force us to find the Lord of Love in a tangible and potent way and fall upon him for healing. Our weaknesses drive us to humility and cause us to look ever deeper for Jesus within his Word. Need for his help motivates us to knock, search, and ask. I have found that, just as he promises, he opens, he reveals, and he gives.

Our frailty drives us to form meaningful relationships with others. Coming face to face with our spiritual infirmities and illnesses serves to reduce the arrogance and the spirit of criticism that inhibit positive connections among us. Personal weaknesses teach us to love and relate to people. As we come to see our own wounds and spiritual inadequacies, we are empowered to see others in their weaknesses without the eye of judgment or a sense of superiority. We may even be able to offer a helping hand. We are all simply God's children and we are all in need of our heavenly Father. We are sheep of the fold, and whether we have wandered away or not, we equally are in need of the guidance of our true Shepherd.

USING THIS BOOK FOR GROUP PRACTICE

My study of these twelve healing miracles has convinced me that Divine Love wants us to participate in and enjoy fellowship with one another. In the Gospels, the Lord of Love tells us that he dwells in the least of his brothers and sisters, which is to say, all of us. He dwells where two or three are gathered together. If each individual has a unique relationship with God, then many individuals will clearly provide a fuller picture of the face and hands of Divine Love. But the union of many is not simply a matter of addition, just as the union of cells and organs of the body is not merely a matter of addition. Something wondrous and more alive than our own selves is created in community. I have found that several of these healings require communication with others to be effective. To this end, the book is designed to be used as guide for weekly spiritual growth groups (though it can also be used by individuals).

Something inside of us resists sharing our deepest thoughts and feelings with others. We don't want to make ourselves vulnerable. We don't want to admit to others our frailty and imperfection. It is possible that we resist community out of a sense of pride. But, as we will discuss later, that very pride is a spiritual weakness. If we are serious about our spiritual progress, in my opinion, it will behoove us to triumph over pride and allow ourselves to experience the Lord's healing in fellowship with other people. Another inhibition we may feel is fear—fear that others will judge and reject us. We fear that if our pretense is let down, we will be socially unacceptable. However, in my experience the opposite has most often proven true. When we are honest with others about our true selves, including our spiritual infirmities, others appreciate it. They feel as if we have honored them with our trust and honesty. They often respond in kind. A powerful fellowship is developed. This is especially true when a group of people have intentionally gathered for the express purpose of supporting one another in spiritual development, as would be the case for those who meet together to work through this book.

Not all readers will be able to access a group due to infirmity or distance from other interested parties. Such individuals may wish to create online groups with friends, or they may contact a spiritually oriented organization such as a church or, if it applies, a twelve-step group to help them set up or join an online group. Alternatively, such a person may wish to work with a selected friend via phone or the Internet. Others may prefer reading and working alone and in prayer with God. Though the offered group activities will be impossible in such cases, I believe benefit can still gained by working through the book solo.

Jesus commands that we wash one another's feet (John 13:14). In the story surrounding that instruction, Jesus tells Peter that he who has been bathed, need not be bathed again, but only have his feet cleansed. Being bathed is a clear reference to being baptized. The washing of feet that we are commanded to do, therefore, in my opinion, is a symbolic command for us to assist one another in keeping ourselves spiritually healthy and clean. Understandably, Peter was embarrassed to show his dirty feet to the Lord. So too, we are embarrassed to discuss our weaknesses with one another. Yet the Lord insisted that he clean Peter's feet and that we do so for one another. When another is in our presence, willing to accept us despite our dirty spiritual feet, it is as if God is before us, because in that person is unconditional love. It is a blessing to both ourselves and the other that we be willing to accept this gift of love.

Groups can be thought of as obedience to the command that we wash one another's feet. We share with one another the emotional and moral dust that has collected upon the feet of our spirit during the week's progress of our spiritual walk. In turn, we accept this honesty of others graciously. We don't turn away and say, "Wow, your feet stink!" Instead, we lovingly apply water and a towel. We listen to others with nonjudgmental compassion. We share our experience of strength and hope.

Like Peter, however, we don't need a full bath. We need not expose before the group all of our past sins, as John required before baptism. Instead we share those troubles and issues that come up in our current spiritual walk. If the burden of past sins is weighing upon us and we need to be cleared of that burden, there is a way of letting go of that burden. Chapter 2 of this book discusses how we can accomplish this.

As we take the spiritual journey of love, more dirt will collect on our feet. In fact, the more we are motivated by love, the more likely we are to find ourselves in challenging situations in the hopes of somehow helping. If we aren't motivated, we won't venture into the murky, muddy areas of life. Remembering this can help us to refrain from judging one another as we go about sharing and listening in the group setting.

After a member shares, I encourage him or her to ask the others for their responses. Group members can then respond with their feelings, thoughts, experiences, and even advice about what has been shared. It takes a level of humility to receive advice from others, but humility is good. The ability to learn from one another is an excellent step in spiritual progress. Advice is somewhat shunned in American culture, but it is a vital and valuable part of many cultures elsewhere around the globe. We bare our spiritual feet not simply to air them, but to have them cleansed by the water—the ideas—of others. If we are going to lower our pride enough to share our weaknesses and shortcomings with others, we might as well be willing to remain humble enough to listen to what others have to say.

I cannot emphasize enough the importance of listening with focused, nonjudgmental empathy, and when we respond to others with a parallel experience or offer a suggestion, that we do so not from a stance of, "I know what is best for you," but rather, "Here's something that crosses my mind and I hope it may be of service to you." When Jesus washed the feet of his disciples, he humbled himself to them. So should we remain humble as listeners.

One final thought about spiritual foot washing before moving on: sandal-clad feet may get dustier and muddier, but they are less prone than sneaker-clad feet to fungal infection and stench. The implication is that if we remain open and honest about our spiritual challenges on a weekly or even daily basis, our problems have less time to fester and breed. It is healthier to be communicative about our troubles and foibles than to try to keep them shoed up. Eventually, the shoe is going to have to come off. Thus I recommend that each member of the group agree to a sharing partnership with one other member of the group. I suggest that the sharing partners agree to contact one another once every day to discuss progress and problems of the past twenty-four hours.

A suggested group format is as follows:

1. Social time (perhaps with snacks, tea, coffee).
2. Opening prayer: All holding hands in a circle, after a moment of silence, each member speaks a short prayer in turn. Alternatively, one member can be elected to speak an opening prayer.
3. Discussion of chapter and personal application throughout the week, using the discussion questions provided if so desired.
4. Closing prayer.

A group may want to choose a facilitator/leader to serve or may prefer a more organic and egalitarian style. Either is fine.

~~~

Many of the lessons prescribed in this book are challenging and require work; sometimes painful work. But the rewards—inner peace, increased sense of love for others, a more tangible sense of God's presence in our lives and all around us, hope, liberation from destructive habits and thoughts, increased joy, an empowerment to effect positive changes in our lives, an increase in awareness—are well worth it.

It is likely that not everyone will connect with this book. Not everyone who encountered Jesus two thousand years ago needed a miracle. In fact, as far as we know, none of the twelve apostles required any healing from him. Likewise, not everyone who approaches Jesus today necessarily needs a lot of spiritual and psychological healing. On the other hand, for those of us who do, this book may be important.

Jesus is real. Through the stories describing how he healed people of their physical infirmities two thousand years ago, he can heal us of spiritual and psychological ailments today. God is present and powerful yesterday, today, and tomorrow the same.

It is my earnest hope that this book might help you and others to more fully know and feel the amazing grace and love of our God, Jesus Christ. It is my joyful opportunity to share some of the ways that the Lord God Jesus Christ has touched my life with his gentle guidance and powerful healing. This book is the realization of three hopes of mine: to proclaim the mercy and joy of the Lord; to help others find healing; and to translate my relationship with the Lord of Love into a meaningful service of love to as many others as possible.

12 Miracles of
Spiritual Growth

1

HEALING FROM FEELINGS

OF UNWORTHINESS

". . . even the dogs eat the crumbs . . ."

Matthew 15:21–28

Jesus left that place and went away to the district of Tyre and Sidon. Just then a Canaanite woman from that region came out and started shouting, "Have mercy on me, Lord, Son of David; my daughter is tormented by a demon."

But he did not answer her at all. And his disciples came and urged him, saying, "Send her away, for she keeps shouting after us."

He answered, "I was sent only to the lost sheep of the house of Israel."

But she came and knelt before him, saying, "Lord, help me." He answered, "It is not fair to take the children's food and throw it to the dogs."

She said, "Yes, Lord, yet even the dogs eat the crumbs that fall from their masters' table."

Then Jesus answered her, "Woman, great is your faith! Let it be done for you as you wish." And her daughter was healed instantly.

"Throw it to the dogs"—I have always found these words, and this whole story, difficult to digest. Why did Jesus call this woman a dog? This doesn't sound like a message from the Lord of Love. Facing this and other such challenging passages can send us spiraling into a whirlpool of doubts. Arriving at the conclusion that the all-loving God couldn't possibly utter such words, we may feel forced to believe either that Jesus didn't actually say these words or that Jesus isn't actually God. In either case, our faith is compromised. We might get so upset at Jesus's words that we overlook the fact that he healed the woman's daughter according to her fervent request.

It is important that we come to understand why Jesus spoke as he did. When we face a difficult story like this, it is an opportunity to increase our conscious contact with God. If left unresolved, doubts in our Lord or his Word will likely dilute our faith. But if we come to see the love and healing within these words, we have grown deeper in trust and understanding of the Lord of Love. This is vital to our spiritual development, and it is also necessary in making our faith living and dynamic. So, why, indeed, did Jesus address this poor woman in such an apparently derogatory manner?

I have found a very useful tool in coming to understand difficult passages in the Word of God, namely to assume a message of love exists in all of scripture and search for that message. We can base our examination of this story on a faith that Jesus is the all-loving God whose essential message is, as he himself states, "Love one another as I have loved you. No one has greater love than this, to lay down one's life for one's friends" (John 15:12–13).

Despite his initial words in this account, Jesus's actions make it obvious that he did indeed love this woman and her daughter. He wanted healing for them. And knowing Jesus to be infinitely more loving and wise than any mere human, we can rest confident that he behaved and spoke in exactly the way that was needed for this healing to take place.

Time and again I have discovered that using a meditative imagination to empathize with the characters of the Bible is a powerful key to unlocking God's messages hidden within. The meaning of this story unveiled itself to me while I was meditating on it. After arriving at a meditative state of mind, I began imagining myself in the place of the Canaanite woman. God desires that we develop empathy, so it is little wonder that searching God's Word with the lens of empathy will yield much fruit. Let's imagine the situation of this poor mother.

Start with the fact that she is a woman—a woman in a culture completely dominated by men. In that culture, women were considered little more than property, servants for men. The primary purpose of marriage was not companionship, but to produce children. The second most important reason for marriage was to increase family wealth and status. A woman was not viewed so much as a human being in her own right, but as a tool for achieving these ends.

It was perfectly acceptable for a displeased husband to divorce his wife (Matt. 19:7–9). There was no concept of commitment on the part of a husband. The fact that a man could for any reason divorce his wife with nothing more than a signature illuminates the negative cultural attitude toward women. Again we see that a wife's value was measured by her capacity to please and serve her husband rather than by her inherent value as a daughter of God.

Further revealing the prevailing derogatory attitude held toward women in ancient Jewish society is the fact that scholars and teachers simply didn't interact with women in public. His disciples were shocked when they found Jesus engaged in conversation with the Samaritan woman by the well (John 4:27). Their upset was in part because she was a non-Jew and in part because she was a woman.

Thus, the Canaanite in the story of our present consideration surely believed herself a second-class citizen at best, simply because she was a woman. She probably valued herself not as a daughter of God, but as a servant to men, the same men who belittled her.

Compounding this woman's sense of insignificance and unworthiness was the fact that she was not a Jew. She was from Canaan, a gentile nation despised by the Jews. She was not of the chosen. As she approached this Jewish man, Jesus, she felt intimidated because she was of the wrong gender, wrong culture, wrong nation, and wrong religion.

As if all of this wasn't enough, there is little doubt that she considered herself flawed and sinful. In ancient cultures people believed that defects and deformities in offspring were the result of the sinfulness of the parents. A demon-possessed child would have likely brought shame to the woman. She may have received silent, condescending disdain from her neighbors or possibly outright blame and cruelty.

Looking at all of these facts, we begin to understand how this woman must have felt about herself. She undoubtedly considered herself to be of little or no value. These general feelings of unworthiness were only compounded by the initial responses she received from the disciples and then Jesus himself. First, she was ignored. Then she was told to go away. She heard the disciples ask Jesus to shoo her off. And then came Jesus's own stinging words, "I was sent only to the lost sheep of the house of Israel."

Amazingly, she still didn't give up. Rather, she worshipped him and begged again. But even this act of devotion only served to elicit the final attack against her sense of worth when Jesus answered her with these searing words, "It is not fair to take the children's food and throw it to the dogs."

Imagine how you would feel if, when you approached your pastor for help, his response was that he didn't have time or desire to help "dogs"? How would you react? Most of us wouldn't deal too well with such words. If at this point the woman had become enraged and left Jesus in self-righteous defiance, we would understand. We would see justification if she had given Jesus a piece of her mind and reprimanded him for being so rude. Would we have done otherwise?

But this woman, amazingly, did no such thing. The vital question for us to ask ourselves is what made this woman so strong. How was she able to rise above the sting of first the disciples' responses to her, and then Jesus's responses? From where did she find the dignity and strength to calmly keep pushing for her cause?

The answer is her passionate love for her daughter. The hope and desire for her daughter's liberation from severe inner torment was so powerful that all other concerns were as nothing in comparison. The potential barriers of fear, sense of inadequacy, indignation, and rage did not distract her from her sole concern. This wonderful woman is inspiring in that she refused to let anything take precedence over her love for her daughter, not even her pride.

And from that love she spoke, "Yes, Lord, yet even the dogs eat the crumbs that fall from their masters' table." We cannot help but feel deep compassion for this woman. And finally Jesus responds to the woman in a new way: "Woman, great is your faith! Let it be done for you as you wish." And her daughter was healed instantly.

Now how does the woman feel? Surely she felt unimaginably elated. She must have wept profusely as she rocked her now-sane daughter within her arms. She must have felt a depth of gratitude to which no words can do justice. And Jesus's message must have rung through her mind over and over again: "Woman, great is your faith! Let it be done for you as you wish."

Jesus didn't just heal her daughter, he healed her. In his final words to her, he obliterated a lifetime of feelings of worthlessness. He showed her that she was powerful—that she was important. He showed her that it was her desire and her faith that enabled the healing. And he showed her all of this in a way that would never allow her to again sink into the same quagmire of shame and feelings of unworthiness. From that moment onward, every time she saw her healed daughter, she would witness the living evidence that she was a worthwhile human being. She would remember that it was her faith and persistence that had facilitated the healing of her daughter. Her healed daughter was proof of the truth of Jesus's encouraging and empowering message to her.

Now we are able to see why Jesus treated this woman with such apparent disdain. Jesus knows the hearts and minds of all of us. He knew Nathaniel before having met him. From the beginning, he knew what Judas would do. He knew of Peter's denial before Peter could even fathom such an act. Jesus knew the entire life history of the woman by the well in Samaria. And surely Jesus knew all about this mother whose daughter was demon-possessed. He knew that she felt very insignificant and worthless—like a little dog. He knew, too, that her love for her daughter was so powerful that she would not accept no for an answer.

Now, having known all of this, what if Jesus had simply said to the woman, "Oh my dear woman. Don't worry. Your daughter is healed. Also, I want you to know that you are a very important and valuable human being." We have to put ourselves in the shoes of the woman. Obviously, we feel grateful for the healing. We feel immensely grateful. But I doubt we feel the overwhelming sense of empowerment that comes only after we tenaciously push through all resistance and obtain our daughter's healing. An easy victory just doesn't carry the punch of one that is grabbed from the jaws of defeat. Jesus wanted her to know this second kind of joy: the joy of overcoming all odds.

And how would we feel about ourselves after Jesus's encouraging words—"I want you to know that you are a very important and valuable human being"? We'd likely feel curious that Jesus offered this kind of emotional bolstering. We would wonder how he knew we held ourselves in low esteem. But because we have felt this way since birth, we ourselves may not even realize how poorly we value ourselves. At any rate, we'd likely feel comforted for a few days, and then the feeling would fade. We'd go back to the self-depreciating attitudes we held before. Words don't pack the punch that experience offers.

What Jesus did was *prove* to the woman her own worthiness and power. He absolutely forced her to exert her strength far beyond what she felt was within her capacity or position. He made her struggle and push even against himself, God. And in the end, he showed her that her faith and love were so powerful that she, like Jacob, could wrestle with both man and God and overcome.

Because of this, he didn't need to *tell* her that she was worthy or powerful; he had proved it to her. She knew it in her heart and there was no denying it. She wasn't a weak and pitiful recipient of the crumbs of mercy from the Healer. On the contrary, she was the strong mother who wrested a blessing out of Jesus by her powerful love and tenacious faith. It was her strength, faith, persistence, and ultimately love that led to the healing of her daughter. And the only way Jesus could have achieved this healing for both the daughter and the mother was in the miraculous and paradoxical way he did it. What looked on the surface like cruelty was an act of deep love—provoking the woman to assert herself.

Simultaneously, Jesus also initiated the healing of society by publicly validating the worth of a woman and of a gentile. He sowed the seeds of change, the fruit of which still grows today throughout the world. Jesus's healing is for all—the daughter, the woman, society, and us today. This story is precisely written to exorcise our minds, today, of the same demon that bodily possessed the little girl then. Jesus's healings transcend time.

By means of this story, we too can access Jesus's healing. Jesus wants to cast out of our lives the demon of feeling worthless and unworthy of God's love. We might call this the "dog" demon. If we feel self-loathing, worthless, depressed, or the like, we can know that this demon has possessed us.

The messages that arise from a feeling of self-loathing are very convincing. Our thoughts tell us that we are worthless, and we wholeheartedly agree with this dismal assessment. Self-hatred captures us, its victims, in such a way that we cannot see any reality outside of that self-hatred. It is therefore impossible to escape self-hatred without external intervention. We need God's help.

When we feel ourselves to be nothing but a little street dog, we aren't able to come to God. I sometimes wonder how many people who drift away from God do so because they subconsciously feel unworthy of God's presence, that is, unworthy of love. But God is for the people, all of us, saints and sinners alike. We don't feel worthy of God's time and attention and so do not approach him—and as a result, we can't be healed. Because we don't approach God, we are unable to contact God's truth, which is that he loves us fully and desires that we feel loved and worthy to be alive. So when we suffer from a sense of worthlessness, we are trapped in a cycle that seems hopeless.

Jesus wants to cast this false notion out of us. This story is the means by which he does it. First, just as Jesus forced the woman to push hard for her healing, so Jesus forces *us* to push hard for our healing. The meaning of this story is not easy to come by. Just to understand the message of this healing, we had to delve deep and push hard. After reading Jesus's harsh words toward the woman, it would be easy—seemingly justifiable—for us to leave off faith in disappointment and upset. But just as the woman's persistence led to a great reward, so our persistence in seeking Jesus's love within this story leads to a great reward in our lives.

By persevering through the surface to the inner message of this story, we suddenly see the astounding depth of Jesus's love. His love is wiser and deeper than we'll ever know. It doesn't matter how unworthy we feel; Jesus's love reaches out to everybody. Just knowing this wins half the battle for us. But merely seeing the love of God within the story isn't enough—there is more. After having pushed through the difficulties of understanding this story, we must again tenaciously push through the difficulties within our own spirits.

When we are possessed by feelings of unworthiness, we are wise to follow the ways of this woman. We need to be persistent in our effort to access Jesus. Like the Canaanite woman, we must desire healing so fervently that we are willing to struggle with God. The Lord tells us in one parable that sometimes it will seem as if he is an uncaring and unjust judge, but that if we are persistent, even such a judge will yield to our desire for justice (Luke 18:1–8).

We should also notice the *way* in which the woman was persistent. She wasn't belligerent or rude about it. Even after Jesus's apparent disregard for her problem, the text shows us that she worshipped him. Only in a worshipful, hopeful approach to Jesus do we access the healing revealed in this story.

Lastly, we should remember the woman's motivation. She succeeded in winning the healing from Jesus because the passionate love she felt for her daughter empowered her. Spiritual healing and growth are inherently based in love. If we think about it rationally, we come to see that a sense of worthlessness hinders our ability to give and receive love. It makes us morose and trapped within ourselves. This state of mind affects those around us negatively. Our sense of worthlessness causes us to medicate our emotions with bad habits and addictions. These, in turn, hurt those around us. When we are tired of hurting those around us, love will lead us to Jesus's healing. If we are tired of the way our self-depreciation inhibits our ability to love and connect with others, if we are saddened by the way our self-hatred affects others negatively, then we will be empowered to tenaciously petition God for healing until we receive what we want. Love will drive us to take God to court, his own court, and quote back to him his own words. We might pray in this way:

Dear Lord Jesus,
You made me. You know everything about me and I admit to you that I feel worthless. I have tried my best and failed. I did not ask to be born like this. I need help! You have promised to help those who come to you. You have promised to be a faithful God. I am knocking on your door. I am seeking for you to be real in my life. I am asking you for help! I can't do this on my own. I don't know what else to do but beg you for help. You must help me. By your very words, you are obliged to help me!

But there is another angle within this story. We read that the disciples were dismissive toward her. Unlike Jesus, they did not heal her daughter. It is likely that they could not have healed her even if they had tried. And unlike Jesus, they were condescending toward her because they believed themselves to be more important and worthy than a Canaanite woman. We see the disciples' propensity for a sense of self-importance in the repeated arguments between the disciples about who would be the greatest among them.

There's a part of us that, like the disciples, feels self-righteous and condescending toward others. This is often true even when we loathe ourselves and deem ourselves unworthy of life. In fact, I have noticed that the two appear to be yoked together. The more I judge others, the more I judge myself. The more I judge myself, the more prone I am to judge others. The two, self-deprecation and disdain for others, are intrinsically united. It is as Jesus said, "Do not judge, so that you may not be judged" (Matt. 7:1). The two attitudes of worthlessness and smugness are bound together in the false notion of hierarchy.

Feelings of worthlessness can only arise when we believe in a hierarchy of humans. But hierarchies don't apply to a person's inherent value. It is manifestly clear that our God, Jesus, loves all people equally. We are all his children. We are all worthy of his love. Jesus does not play favorites or withhold his infinite love from anyone for any reason. Think of the prodigal son. When we know that there is no hierarchy, that we are all equally made in God's image and likeness, then we know that we are neither less worthy nor more worthy of God's love, healing, and life.

So part of the healing Jesus is offering us in this story is contained within the truth that all human beings are equally God's beloved children—Jew and gentile, man and woman, healthy and ill, disciple and non-disciple. This truth not only heals us of feeling like a little dog, it also empowers us to love other people without reservation.

The woman was suffering under a society based in hierarchy. Males, Jews, and healthy specimens were at the top of the heap. Non-Jewish women with sick daughters were at the bottom. Jesus proved to her that the societal hierarchical beliefs were totally false. Many of us suffer under a different internal hierarchy. We may believe that people who are successful are more "valuable," which, when we think about it, means more worthy of life and God's love.

Or maybe we believe that people of a certain faith or culture are at the top of God's list. We may believe that people who are emotionally and spiritually strong are better than those who are weak. When our consciousness is ordered in a hierarchical way, we suffer the plight of this woman. We at some level feel unworthy of even of being alive. We feel like a little dog. And this diseased attitude is just like the demon that possessed the little girl.

This miracle has shown us how to let Jesus heal us of a constitutional sense of worthlessness. This is the first detailed account of a healing in the New Testament, and this is also the first miracle that must take place in our lives as we progress along the lines of spiritual growth and healing. Shattering the delusion that we are unworthy of God is ground zero for our spiritual journey. Breaking the delusion that humans exist in a hierarchy of value is essential for this to occur. Until the notion that we are unworthy of God and life is dispelled, we can't move forward. We need to be able to approach God if we intend to receive his help with our problems.

The truth is that we are all God's children. We are all his beloved. We are worthy of a rich, joyful life based upon true union with him and others around us. We are all worthy of God's love and worthy of life!

I well recall the moment the constant self-disparaging self-talk that plagued me for years was dramatically silenced. That experience opened up into two weeks of the most potent spiritual sense of awakening I have ever had. I pray that if you too suffer from a "little dog" spirit, you might be healed so that you can accept yourself and awaken to the palpable presence of Divine Love permeating all of life.

MEDITATIONS

1. After entering into a meditative state of mind (see appendix), search for and focus on any feelings of unworthiness. After some time, imagine yourself as the Canaanite woman with the demon-possessed daughter. Imagine your daughter as vividly as possible.

First, see yourself holding her as a tiny, normal infant; then as a happy toddler. Build your feelings of love for her to be as powerful as possible. Now see her as seven-year-old looking with love into your eyes and running up to you for your embrace. Hold her with your love. Now see her at age twelve. She curses and thrashes. She mutilates herself. Feel the depth of sorrow that your wondrous daughter has been seized by a demon. Get in touch with the emotions that flow through the story—the tender love for your daughter; the sense of desperation; the mounting determination.

Now relive this story as vividly and fully as possible from the perspective of the Canaanite woman. See the dusty roads and the press of people. Hear the noises; feel the heat and bumping crowd. What smells do you encounter? Make it real. You bring your daughter toward Jesus. His followers tell you to go away. You cry out for mercy, but Jesus ignores you, and the disciples tell Jesus to make you go away. You hear Jesus say, "I was sent only to the lost sheep of Israel." But you bow down and worship Jesus and say, "Please help me!" You hear Jesus say, "It is not fair to take the children's food and throw it to the dogs." You reply, "Yes Lord, but even the dogs eat the crumbs that fall from their masters' table." You suddenly feel a change within your spirit—you feel Jesus's presence within and you hear him confirming this feeling. "Woman, great is your faith! Let it be done for you as you wish."

You look at your daughter and she is clearly healed. She is smiling and laughing even as tears are flowing down her face. Your tears flow too as you embrace her. She is back with you, restored to her former self.

2. Again after entering into a meditative state of mind, focus on the singular truth that the Lord loves you and all people infinitely and perfectly.

LEAVES

1. You are loved infinitely by the Lord. You are created to be loved and so love.

2. Sometimes love masks itself to accommodate and best serve us in our current state.

3. There is no hierarchy of human value. All of us are equally loved and important.

FRUIT

1. As a way of identifying and exposing the "dog demon," write down all the self-belittling messages that are repeated or stored up inside of your mind. Write down all the reasons you don't like yourself.

2. Write down all the ways that this self-hatred affects those around you.

3. Come to a decision that for their sakes and for yours, you want healing and are willing to do whatever it takes to extract it from God.

4. Make a list of the ways in which you have thought of human beings as existing along a hierarchy of value (e.g., people who sin are less valuable than those who do not; people who are accomplished are better than those who are not accomplished).

5. Throughout the week, notice all the times you begin thinking in terms of one of these false hierarchies and then replace these thoughts with the fact that all humans are equally valuable and worthy of the love.

6. Repeat this or a similar prayer daily or as needed:
"Lord, I am suffering from a demon that makes me feel unworthy of love, unworthy of life, unworthy of you and your healing. I cannot overcome this demon by myself. I am your child. You have promised to not leave us as orphans. I am sick and need your healing. You have promised to give to those who ask. I am asking, Lord, that you heal me of this false feeling that I am worthless. I pray for my own sake, but I also pray for the sake of those around me who are negatively affected by my sense of worthlessness. Lord, show me you love me. Let me feel your love for me. Thank you, Lord Jesus."

7. Contact your phone partner midweek and talk about how the process of this healing is going.

DISCUSSION QUESTIONS

1. Has anything remarkable happened to you this week; did the Lord touch you this week in a special way concerning or not concerning the message of this miracle?

2. Have you ever had an experience where you felt insulted or belittled by someone of a "higher" status? How did you respond? How do you see that situation now?

3. What was your experience of the meditations? How did it feel when Jesus turned you away? How did it feel when you persisted and your daughter was healed?

4. What was your experience of the exercises? Did you find any of them particularly helpful or meaningful? If so, why?

5. If any value was gained from this miracle, how can we incorporate it and sustain it in our daily lives?

6. How can we support one another in relation to this miracle?

2

HEALING FROM LACK OF FORGIVENESS

"Son, your sins are forgiven."

Mark 2:1–12

When he returned to Capernaum after some days, it was reported that he was at home. So many gathered around that there was no longer room for them, not even in front of the door; and he was speaking the word to them.

Then some people came, bringing to him a paralyzed man, carried by four of them. And when they could not bring him to Jesus because of the crowd, they removed the roof above him; and after having dug through it, they let down the mat on which the paralytic lay. When Jesus saw their faith, he said to the paralytic, "Son, your sins are forgiven."

Now some of the scribes were sitting there, questioning in their hearts, "Why does this fellow speak in this way? It is blasphemy! Who can forgive sins but God alone?"

At once Jesus perceived in his spirit that they were discussing these questions among themselves; and he said to them, "Why do you raise such questions in your hearts? Which is easier, to say to the paralytic, 'Your sins are forgiven,' or to say, 'Stand up and take your mat and walk?' But so that you may know that the

Son of Man has authority on earth to forgive sins"—he said to the paralytic—"I say to you, stand up, take your mat and go to your home."

And he stood up, and immediately took the mat and went out before all of them; so that they were all amazed and glorified God, saying, "We have never seen anything like this!"

~~~

In most cases of paralysis the brain is in good condition and has messages to send the body, and the body is also fit, able to execute the commands of the brain. The problem arises because of a failure in communication between the head and the body due to nerve damage in the neck. People who believe in Jesus as Lord often refer to themselves as "the body of Christ" and understand Jesus to be the head of that body. In this miracle we see the same problem replicated in a fractal-like manner on three levels of reality. Just as communication between the paralytic's brain and body was blocked, so communication between Christ and the man as a member of the body of Christ was physically blocked by the pressing throng, which he could not get through. These are the first two parallel replications of the same problem. The third way communication failure is expressed within this miracle is by the unforgiving spirit of the Pharisees. The false belief that sins cannot be forgiven blocks us from sensing God's communications with us. Until we arrive at a state of forgiveness, we are severed from feeling God's presence in our lives. This miracle is Jesus's way of healing us of this form of spiritual paralysis.

"Who can forgive sins but God alone?" It would seem that these are the words of a callous, uncaring heart, and yet many of us have a similar voice sounding in our own consciousness. We want people to pay for their misdeeds in full—especially those whose actions harmed us personally. Someone aggravates us. We mentally review the interaction over and over, enforcing our rightness and the other party's wrongness. Maybe we even imagine revenge scenarios or future arguments in which we really cut the other down to size. Every time we hold a grudge like this, we can know that the Pharisees of our heart are hard at work. In holding a grudge, we are cut off from communication with God. Our condemning attitude and God's forgiving love are mutually exclusive.

Sometimes this unforgiving voice targets other people. But just as often, it is ourselves we refuse to forgive. We did something we knew was wrong. We hurt someone or we betrayed our own sense of what is right. We are dismayed or maybe even horrified, and we choose not to forgive ourselves. Frequently, we don't even know how to forgive ourselves. We are paralyzed.

On the natural level—that is, if you read the words literally—this is a story about healing from paralysis and about forgiveness. In the internal, spiritual level, these two issues are one and the same. Guilt causes paralysis of the spirit. To receive God's forgiveness is to be healed and released into freedom again. This miracle is Christ's way of dissipating our guilt and restoring us into a meaningful relationship with him.

In this chapter we learn to let Jesus heal us from paralyzing guilt. We learn to let the Lord forgive and love us, despite our past faults. This and the previous healing are similar, but there is an important difference. In the first story, Jesus heals us of constitutional self loathing. These negative feelings and opinions we have about ourselves are based not on our deeds, but on a fundamental false belief that at our core we are worthless and unworthy of life. In this second story, Jesus is offering us healing and freedom from the crippling guilt that arises from genuine and specific misdeeds and sins.

I would like to distinguish between healthy guilt and pathological guilt. I've heard some people say all guilt is bad. I don't espouse this belief. Guilt is the spiritual equivalent to pain. Neither feels good, but both are necessary. Just as physical pain serves to prevent us from hurting our own bodies, so guilt is the spiritual pain we need to prevent us from hurting the communal body we call society. Sociopaths are characterized by a complete lack of guilt. Guilt is an emotion that keeps us on track and keeps society together. What is not good, however, is paralyzing guilt. Guilt becomes crippling and pathological when we fail to process and move beyond guilt in appropriate ways. This pathological guilt is actually an unforgiving spirit that is directed toward self. This is the kind of guilt that is unhealthy and from which this miracle heals us.

When we hold a grudge against ourselves, we are stuck in an impossible situation. We mercilessly require of ourselves that which we cannot give—a new past. We simply cannot erase the reality that we have made mistakes. So long as we refuse to forgive ourselves and grow beyond the past, the Pharisaical aspect of our mind whips and thrashes us relentlessly. If we could see our spiritual reality, we would see that internally we are precisely like the paralyzed man. Our guilt immobilizes us. We cannot grow. We cannot rejoice. We cannot bless others. The reason is that we have lost communication with that which causes us to grow, rejoice, and bless—the Lord of Love.

Guilt stunts our relationship with God and others. We become fixated on our inadequacy and fault. Our ability to share God's joy with others is annihilated because we have no joy to share. We become morose and even suicidal. The spiritual faculties needed to touch and affect others for good are, as it were, paralyzed and useless. This kind of self-condemnation severely compromises our ability to love and appreciate others.

The unforgiving Pharisees were considered the authorities on God. What they said was taken as true and was to be obeyed. Similarly, we often imagine that God wants us to soak in guilt and self-condemnation. We are listening to our internal Pharisees, mistaking them to be the spokesmen of God. So it is important for us to see that self-condemnation and paralyzing guilt are not God's will—on the contrary, these attitudes and feelings stifle God's ability to work through us. Just the realization that excessive guilt hampers our ability to participate in God's plan of love helps begin the healing process. Our desire to be close to God and to serve him requires that we move beyond guilt.

In this biblical account, the men couldn't reach Jesus except by the roof because of the crowd. The crowd consisted mostly of people who loved Jesus and wanted to hear him. We can think of the crowd of eager listeners as an internal aspect of our own being—the part of us that is eager to know God and do what is right. Just as the crowd of believers prevented the man from reaching Jesus, so our desire to love and serve God often blocks our ability to receive his forgiveness and healing. Feelings of guilt arise only in context of the desire to do what is right, to love others and to serve God. If we didn't in some way love God and other people, we would not experience guilt. So guilt, even though not in itself healthy, is actually a good sign. If we are paralyzed by guilt, we can take heart.

We cannot simply say, "OK, I know God forgives me! I'm not going to feel guilty anymore!" and be cleansed of guilt. If it were that easy, it wouldn't actually be guilt. Of ourselves, we have no more power to vanquish guilt than the paralytic had to get up and walk before encountering Jesus. But the man and his friends did have faith, we read. We read that Christ forgave the man his sins after having seen his faith and that of his friends.

Do we have faith in Jesus? Who is Jesus? Jesus's final commandment sums up his entire message: "This is my commandment, that you love one another as I have loved you. No one has greater love than this, to lay down one's life for one's friends" (John 15:12–13). Thus when we ask ourselves if we believe in Jesus, we are really asking ourselves if we believe in Divine Love. Do we believe that Divine Love is real? Do we believe that Divine Love is what makes us truly human and so is the essence of our true humanity? Being the essence of our true humanity, do we recognize that Divine Love, therefore, is more alive and more human than we are as individuals? Thus do we admit that Divine Love is the author of our humanity and is divine? Do we believe that by following the dictates of Divine Love we will come to know true peace and joy—in a word, heaven? Seeing that Love is more human, more real, and more alive than we are, can we believe that Love is a sentient being who seeks to communicate with us? And in seeking to communicate with us, can we believe that this Lord of Love took on a body so as to break through a communication blockage that had begun to paralyze the human race? To believe in Jesus is to believe that we are loved and also that our salvation lies in learning how to love. This is the motivation we need to move beyond pathological guilt. Like the paralyzed man and his friends, we need to make faith in the Lord of Love our top priority.

Love is not a static entity. To have faith in the Lord of Love is to take action. And if we take the actions of love in relation to our guilty conscience, we will find ourselves propelled toward Jesus and eventually healed.

The man in the story was carried by four friends. We can think of these four friends as four activities that are dictated by love in the context of guilt. If we love someone and we have hurt them, we will want to do these four things. And even if we don't love them, but believe in Love as an ideal, we will still want to do them. I call them the four A's:

1. Admit
2. Apologize
3. Amend
4. Absolve

These four faithful and faith-filled friends will carry us to healing.

1. Admit our Wrongs

First of all, we need to admit to our mistakes and sins. Until we face our wrongs and fully acknowledge our fault, the communication lines between God and ourselves will remain blocked by our denial. We cannot experience the Lord's forgiveness for deeds we don't admit to doing. Sometimes we are so ashamed of our sins that we have difficulty admitting them even to ourselves. So it is doubly important to get down on our knees, and tell God the exact nature of our wrongdoing. It helps restore our relationship not only with God, but with ourselves as well.

Often times, admitting our faults to God within our thoughts or prayers is not a meaningful experience. This is especially true if we have been dwelling on our misdeeds. So where do we meet God more really and fully than within our thoughts? Jesus tells us: he lives within others. He also adds that where two or three are gathered together in his name, there he is in the midst of them. It is best to confess to the person we harmed, unless to do so will cause more harm. Sometimes we have sinned against people without their awareness. In these cases, we must carefully consider the value of a confession. The goal of mending our wrongs is to stop hurting others and start blessing them. On occasion, rather than a confession, it may be wiser to engage in loving actions that stem from a change of heart.

When admitting our wrongs to the harmed person is not possible or would only make matters worse, we can choose a third party. Just as multitudes of people confessed their sins to John the Baptist and so cleared the way for Jesus's ministry in their lives, so we today can open the door for Jesus's ministry in our lives by confessing our sins in the presence of a trustworthy, God-fearing human being who has our best interest in mind. We may wish to confess both to the people we harmed and also to a third party.

Fear of telling the truth even to one who will be supportive is a strong indication that we are still judging ourselves. It is from this very self-condemnation that we are trying to heal. We let Jesus begin the process of healing by acting not as self-condemnation would have us—keeping silent—but in opposition to what self-condemnation dictates: we tell the truth.

We must be very careful in deciding whom to entrust with our confession. We must choose a person who will not betray our trust. We are looking for someone who will understand that we are trying to become better people of God and who will be supportive and eager to help us in this challenging adventure. A prayer or accountability partner will do. A spouse or a trusted pastor or other religious leader can be a good choice. If you are reading this book in the context of a group and feel a sense of trust, it may be the group as a whole or an individual member of the group. If we are in recovery, a twelve-step sponsor is also an excellent choice to serve the role of John the Baptist in our journey toward the Lord's healing. With whomever we choose to confess, it may be wise to complete the act of confession with a baptism ceremony marking an end of the old life and the beginning of a new. Such a ceremony can be very powerful.

We confess our sins not to humiliate ourselves, but to get honest and let fresh air into our spirit. If we have chosen wisely, the recipient of our confession will hear us without judgment or disdain. What we expected to be hideously unpleasant turns out to be liberating and vivifying. We begin to feel tingling in our spiritual limbs; we feel as if we may soon walk again.

2. Apologize

After we admit our wrongs, we then express our regret in the form of an apology. We apologize not to get into the other party's good graces, but to express our true remorse and intention to improve. The response is none of our business. Many times, an apology will be met with forgiveness. Occasionally we will be rejected with hostility or coldness. The Lord of Love, however, is always forgiving us and constantly yearning for our return just as the father yearned for his prodigal son in Jesus's parable. Even when our apology is not accepted by the other party, we can know that we have done our best and that we are forgiven by God.

3. Amend our wrongs

Unless confession and apology are accompanied by the hard work of making amends, little good is likely accomplished. Without taking steps to right our wrongs, the first two steps often amount to a selfish attempt to feel better. Actions to restore what we damaged prove that we have the other party's best interest in mind. We are making sacrifices for the sake of others. This proves to ourselves, to others, and to God that we genuinely regret our misdeeds and are seeking a new way of life. The difficult actions of making amends allow us to trust that our motivation is sincerely to bless those we've hurt and refrain from doing any more harm.

If we have stolen, we compensate for the stolen goods—we overcompensate if we can. Overcompensation in such cases is actually not overcompensation, but a way of making up for the spiritual wrong we have committed; a way of showing our sincere desire to make good. If we have lied, we explain the truth. If we have been cold toward someone, we may want to complement our verbal amends with a gift or by spending time with that individual. In short, we should expand our verbal apology with sincere acts of generosity and love. An action of love fills out and makes the verbal apology real.

We may be paralyzed by guilt over one specific incident. Of course we need to make amends concerning that particular wrongdoing, but we should not stop there. Once we've begun clearing out the closet of our souls, why stop when it is only half clean? We might as well correct everything we can from our past. The more wrongs we make right, the more healed and closer to Jesus we will grow. Our lives will fill with light, love, and peace. Once we have felt the joy of making wrongs right, we likely will be filled with a spiritual urge to keep clearing out our skeletons until there are none left.

4. Absolve All

The fourth and final friend that carries us to Jesus's healing is to forgive all people and rid ourselves of all resentments. Pathological guilt and resentment are two faces of the same coin: an unforgiving spirit. We can't rid ourselves of self-condemnation while clinging to a judgmental spirit. Our goal is to pitch the coin of judgment out of our lives completely. In the Lord's prayer we recite, "Forgive us our trespasses, as we also forgive those who trespass against us." Jesus once told a parable about a man whose master forgave him an enormous debt (Matt. 18:23–35). The forgiven man immediately went out and threw a fellow servant into prison over a relatively tiny debt. Hearing about this incident, the master became enraged and imprisoned the man who had been forgiven. God never imprisons or tortures us, but an unforgiving spirit within us will lead us straight into an imprisoned and tortured state of mind. That is the message of the parable. The forgiveness we might have received from the Lord cannot be accessed by a heart that is smoldering with resentment. The resentment severs the nerve that would otherwise communicate love and forgiveness from the Lord to us as the body of Christ. Thus, to judge others invariably results in self-condemnation. "Do not judge, so that you may not be judged. For with the judgment you make you will be judged, and the measure you give will be the measure you get" (Matt. 7:1–2). This statement of Jesus is literal. Only when we offer forgiveness do we discover that we are forgiven.

To further explain this concept, we can think of forgiveness as a spiritual force from God that is greater than personality and so transcends us. If we accept this spirit of forgiveness into our lives, it animates us in relation to all people—including ourselves—regardless of personhood. Likewise, a judgmental spirit is a destructive spiritual force greater than ourselves, and it too operates regardless of person. If we invite it in against others, it builds a home in our heart and eventually attacks us too.

The process of letting go of resentments requires that we forgive. To forgive, we have to admit that we've been hurt. Sometimes we may pretend that we haven't really been injured. "Oh, I'm not mad. That didn't hurt me." We deceive ourselves that we are tough and beyond getting upset. Or we may say to ourselves, "The past is the past, why dwell on it?" In both cases, we may be denying that inside we are hurting. When on the cross, Jesus didn't say, "I'm tougher than this, so I'm not going to let it get to me!" On the contrary, he called out in agony, "My God, my God, why have you forsaken me?" In admitting his pain and his fear that even God had abandoned him, he prayed for the forgiveness of those who so hurt him. This is an extreme example, but it serves to make a point: we can't truly forgive unless we admit that we have been hurt in the first place.

We need to spend time considering our hurt feelings. To help us do this, we make a list of all the issues over which we are hurting inside. It can be very liberating to do this. Many times, when I am upset, I have no idea what's really wrong. I can't fix the upset and resentment before I know over what issue I'm upset. The process of writing seems to help me identify the events that caused the feelings. We need not deny our feelings, even if they are irrational. We may think, "Oh, I shouldn't be angry about such a small thing." Getting angry isn't the problem. Holding the anger and acting on it are the problems.

After we list our hurt feelings, we then list the people and institutions against whom we hold a grudge or who trigger feelings of pain. Finally, we start praying for a forgiving spirit in relation to each one. We also pray for the well-being of each person and institution. When we pray for the well-being of others, our resentments have no room within our spirits. We keep praying daily until the icy resentments thaw and the hot pain of the past cools. If we are earnest, God will always heal us from past pain and from resentments. Prayer for a forgiving spirit is a prayer that God is very eager to answer. If all else fails, we can even do a deed of kindness to the person we resent.

Another useful tool in overcoming resentment is to remember our own faults in general, and also in relation to the specific person we resent. When we remember our own weaknesses and need for God's mercy, it is much easier for us to find forgiveness for the weaknesses and faults of others. Finally, recalling that those who harm others are acting from their own pain and delusion is very effective in producing a gentler attitude toward others. People who are hurting and damaged tend to hurt others.

The paralytic could not meet Jesus without the aid of his friends. Likewise, we can't simply will away the feelings of overwhelming guilt, but we can take these four steps: 1) Admit our wrongs; 2) Apologize; 3) Amend our wrongs; 4) Absolve all who have harmed us. All of these steps force us to improve our relationships with others. Just as the paralytic's four friends lifted him up above the pressing crowd, these actions lift us up above the pathological guilt. They give us a heightened, transcendent perspective on our previous mindset of self-condemnation. Ultimately, like the four friends, these actions deliver us to the Lord's healing and forgiveness. Whenever we feel guilt cropping up in our hearts, we can employ the four A's.

When I was a child, I was tormented by pathological guilt because I had on one occasion deceived and belittled a peer. In retrospect, I see the hurt I had caused was not nearly so severe as my internal punishment. Nevertheless, I obsessed about my mistake every day for years. This guilt tainted my ability to relate with others, with God, and with myself. This is no way to live. I was paralyzed with guilt. I needed forgiveness. And all of us, when in the grip of crippling guilt, are in desperate need of Jesus's healing mercy.

Several years after the incident, I watched *Flatliners,* a film about a group of med students who induced near-death experiences upon one another in order to explore the afterlife. The main theme and message of the film was that unamended wrongdoing makes for an unpleasant afterlife (as well as current life on earth). Making amends was the only way to clear the way of happiness and peace.

The movie had a profound impact on me. I resolved to make amends to the peer whom I had hurt. The peer couldn't even recall the event. Nevertheless, I clearly remember the palpable sensation of relief. It was as if a massive load had lifted off my shoulders the very moment I made the amends. It was an amazing experience of liberation. I felt alive and free in a way I hadn't known for years. I was happy again.

The Lord is the source of all forgiveness. Even though it seems as if our actions pave the way for relief of guilt, the four A's are all the natural result of putting our faith in the Lord of Love. Thus it is Jesus who is motivating us to take these actions. He allows us to forgive, and he allows us to be forgiven. Jesus told the scribes that the Son of Man has power to forgive. In one sense, we are all sons and daughters of man. That's exactly what we are. So here, Jesus is telling us that forgiving each other is certainly an activity in which we both can and should engage.

Here, as in the previous miracle, we see that Jesus's healing is effective on many planes of reality simultaneously. He healed the man of physical paralysis. Simultaneously, he also began to heal society of the false, paralyzing notion that we can't or shouldn't forgive people. And, of course, within this miraculous account, Jesus reaches out through time and space to heal us, too. He shows us how to find his forgiveness. He shows us how to forgive others and so be relieved of the burden of resentment. He frees us from spiritual paralysis.

MEDITATION

After entering into a meditative state, turn your attention inward. Get in touch with feelings of unresolved guilt and wrongdoing. Now imagine yourself as paralyzed. You see a crowd gathering and realize that the Lord is in the midst of the people. You yearn to meet him. You believe that he can save you. You feel the agony, irony, and frustration of being paralyzed. Your friend is by your side and you beg him to help you meet the Lord. He calls three others who are standing nearby and they begin to carry you on a makeshift stretcher. Unable to penetrate the throng, they carry you to the back of the house. One of your friends slings you over his shoulder as the other three climb up a ladder to the top of the house. They reach down and you are hoisted to the top of the house. Your heart begins to beat faster as you anticipate that you are actually going to encounter the one who can heal you. Your friends begin removing the terracotta tiles and make a hole in the roof. On your bed, you cannot see below as you are lowered into the room. Then suddenly you are face-to-face with the Lord of Love. You know instantly that you will walk again. You hear him say, "Son, your sins are forgiven." You hear these words, but you also hear a voice inside protesting the idea that you can be forgiven for the things you have done to harm others. You then hear the Lord speak again, "Why do you raise such questions in your heart? Which is easier, to say, 'Your sins are forgiven,' or to say, 'Stand up and take your mat and walk?' But so that you may know that the Son of Man has authority on earth to forgive sins, I say to you, stand up, take your mat and go to your home."

On his command, you stand up from the bed. Allow yourself to act spontaneously and do whatever you would like to do in response to your friends' help and having been healed by Jesus of paralysis.

LEAVES

1. Judging others interferes with our ability to feel the Lord's love in our lives.

2. The Lord doesn't desire that we hate ourselves or require that we carry around heavy burdens of guilt.

3. The Lord always has forgiveness for us.

4. Judgment against others and against self are intrinsically united.

5. We have to take certain steps—the four A's—in relation to other people to access freedom from guilt.

6. We must forgive others in order to experience forgiveness ourselves.

FRUIT

1. **Admit** our wrongs to ourselves, to God, to those we harmed (except when to do so will cause more harm), and to a trustworthy witness. We list all of our wrongs, so that we don't gloss over anything.

2. **Apologize** for our wrongdoings.

3. **Amend** our wrongdoings as fully as possible. Overcompensating is expected.

4. **Absolve** all those individuals and institutions who have harmed us or against whom we hold a grudge.

- We list our hurt feelings.
- We list those individuals and institutions who have hurt us and also those against whom we hold a grudge.
- We pray for their well-being and also for a spirit of forgiveness.

5. Contact your phone partner midweek and discuss the experience of this healing. If you are not working with a group, then you might discuss your experience with a trusted friend or family member, or write about it in a personal journal.

DISCUSSION QUESTIONS

1. What was your experience of the meditation?
2. What was your experience of admitting your wrongs?
3. What was your experience of apologizing and making amends?
4. What was your experience of absolving all resentments?
5. Do you find it hard to forgive others? Yourself? Which is harder for you?
6. How can we support one another in continuing the healing offered by this miracle?

3

HEALING FROM SPIRITUAL SLAVERY

"Come out of the man, you unclean spirit!"

Mark 5:1–20

They came to the other side of the sea, to the country of the Gerasenes. And when he had stepped out of the boat, immediately a man out of the tombs with an unclean spirit met him. He lived among the tombs; and no one could restrain him any more, even with a chain; for he had often been restrained with shackles and chains, but the chains he wrenched apart, and the shackles he broke in pieces; and no one had the strength to subdue him. Night and day among the tombs and on the mountains he was always howling and bruising himself with stones.

When he saw Jesus from a distance, he ran and bowed down before him; and he shouted at the top of his voice, "What have you to do with me, Jesus, Son of the Most High God? I adjure you by God, do not torment me!" For he had said to him, "Come out of the man, you unclean spirit!"

Then Jesus asked him, "What is your name?"

He replied, "My name is Legion; for we are many." He begged him earnestly not to send them out of the country. Now there on the hillside a great herd of swine was feeding; and the unclean spirits begged him, "Send us into the swine; let us enter them." So he gave them permission. And the unclean spirits came out and entered the swine; and the herd, numbering about two thousand, rushed down the steep bank into the sea, and were drowned in the sea.

The swineherds ran off and told it in the city and in the country. Then people came to see what it was that had happened. They came to Jesus and saw the demoniac sitting there, clothed and in his right mind, the very man who had had the legion; and they were afraid. Those who had seen what had happened to the demoniac and to the swine reported it. Then they began to beg Jesus to leave their neighborhood.

As he was getting into the boat, the man who had been possessed by demons begged him that he might be with him. But Jesus refused, and said to him, "Go home to your friends, and tell them how much the Lord has done for you, and what mercy he has shown you." And he went away and began to proclaim in the Decapolis how much Jesus had done for him; and everyone was amazed.

~~~~~~

So intense was the misery this demon-possessed man endured on a daily basis that it may be difficult for us to fathom his plight. He was forced to share his mind with a hoard of devils so powerful that they could use his body to snap away chains and shackles. There were so many of these demons that they were able to control a herd of swine numbering over two thousand. And the fact that they instantly and easily overpowered that strongest and most basic instinct of self-preservation within the pigs again shows the awesome strength of these spirits. Little wonder the man's personal will was bound and rendered impotent by the presence of Legion dwelling within him. Against his own will and better judgment, the man sliced and gouged himself with rocks, day and night. This man was enslaved to an evil force; a pawn to their destructive whims.

Yet, taking an honest look at ourselves, many of us come to realize that our personal internal situation is not drastically different from this man's. There could be no better depiction of addiction than the man possessed by Legion. The following chapter will deal specifically with addiction and how we can allow Jesus to heal us of addiction. Though some readers may not consider themselves addicted to anything, I believe this chapter can be useful to all. There are many hidden and subtle forms of addiction. We can become driven by obsession and compulsion in just about any area of life.

The original Latin *addictus*, from which the word addiction is derived, means "one who has been given up or made over as servant to his creditor." We can therefore think of a victim of addiction as having been made servile in relation to an external force, just as the man in the story was given over to Legion. While addiction is traditionally a word reserved for the habitual abuse of a substance such as alcohol or drugs, the meaning of the word has more recently expanded to include habitual destructive activities driven by obsessive thoughts and overpowering desires. Addiction to sex, gambling, and food are commonly accepted concepts these days.

For the purpose of this book, I would like to further broaden the definition of addiction to include any pattern of thought or behavior that we have difficulty eliminating from our lives, and that is detrimental to well-being—both our own and that of those around us. Habitual criticizing, verbal cruelty, an insatiable desire for success at any cost, pessimism, materialism, arrogance, sloth, lust for power, and the like can all be considered addictions in the context of this chapter. The key element of addiction is that our will is given over and enslaved to an external force. This servitude is often so subtle that we fail to distinguish our will from that of the external force.

For example, if we are in the habit of making sarcastic remarks, we likely sense this to be our true self, our own will. Somewhere along the way, we witnessed or were the recipient of sarcasm. We learned to be sarcastic and it became a habit. Once such a habit becomes entrenched into our repertoire of behaviors, we come to view the behavior as an aspect of our true personality. We may even come to take delight in the habit. However, having been made in the image and likeness of God, our truest and inmost soul and will cannot be any other than love. Thus any thought or activity that is not of love is motivated by an external force. It has been acquired either through biological heredity or by experience and example.

In our current era, where scientific thought reigns as the dominant discourse, it is difficult for us to relate to the idea of evil spirits, let alone demonic possession. But perhaps our current spiritual and psychological maladies aren't so different than the possession described in this healing story. Unbeknownst to the majority of us, we are all driven by the spirits of the past. We learn patterns of behavior, thought, and social interaction from our elders. They in turn are, for the most part, repeating the same patterns that they absorbed from their elders.

Massive cultural traumas, such as the genocide of the Native Americans or the enslavement and dehumanization of Africans in the New World, have far-reaching effects that are passed on from generation to generation, a phenomenon referred to as historical trauma. Though many of us are not recipients of such massive trauma loads, none of us can escape the burden of the failures of our ancestors. The sins of the fathers will be visited upon the children to the third and fourth generations (Exod. 20:5).

The innocence into which we are born is coated over and becomes filtered by all of our life experiences. If we experience sarcasm, we are likely to become sarcastic or associate with those who are. If we receive abuse, we are likely to become abusive or associate ourselves with an abuser. If we are exposed to depression, we are likely to be depressed or form bonds with those who are. We subjectively sense these patterns of thought and behavior as innate aspects of our being. I believe, however, that these are learned behaviors. They are external historical forces. They are the spirits of the past living within and animating us. We are all host to a legion of spirits from the past. *Spirit* is an appropriate word for these historical forces that animate us.

Many of these spirits are not conducive to our well-being. And yet so long as they are wedded to our sense of self and will, we have no chance of changing or expelling them on our own power. We need to somehow access the salvation of the Lord of Love.

As this chapter and the following two will show, it is by our imperfection that we come to know the Lord's perfection; by our spiritual illness, his healing; by our disquiet and pain, his peace and joy; by our selfishness, his selfless love. Some readers may suffer or have suffered a more obvious form of addiction. Some may suffer a more subtle form of possession—pessimism, for example. If we have actively chosen to walk with God, that walk will force us to face some of these inner demons. And while the level of destruction and chaos in our lives may be different, the point is that we all equally need God to overcome the possession of our will. Finding our particular weaknesses of will can help awaken within us a true longing for his salvation.

When trapped in addiction, subtle or blatant, there is a part of us that wants out—we want to be healed. We don't want to eat that second piece of pie. We don't want to snipe at our children or spouse with snide comments. We don't want to work overtime every day, leaving us with no family time. We don't want to be depressed. We don't want to prowl the Internet for porn, or place that bet, or drink that scotch. But these good impulses to escape the addiction are dwarfed by the power of the possessing forces, just as the man's own personality and will were rendered impotent by the presence of Legion. Through this story, Jesus, the Lord of Love, reaches out to liberate us from those powers that enslave us in destructive habits.

The spirits caused the man to abuse himself with stones even as he moaned and cried out in agony. Likewise, we moan with anguish as we watch ourselves sink further into self-destructive behavior. For example, the adulterer hates himself for cheating on his wife. He sees his family falling apart. He sees his kids drifting away. He hates the feelings of emptiness and disconnection that arise from his dishonesty and betrayal. And yet to his horror, he finds himself repeating the same sins over and over. The bulimic hates her habit and herself because of it. She's not sure which she hates more. All she knows is that she is utterly ashamed of her behavior and wants to be rid of it at any cost. She even contemplates suicide as an escape from her tormented life. But despite her best efforts, she can't stop gorging and purging. Nor can the anorexic person find the will to eat.

The man possessed by Legion lived among the tombs. This fact is mentioned no less than three times within the first four sentences. When enslaved by forces outside of our true will, it is as if we are dead. We have no freedom and no joy. We have no perception of love or warmth. Looking at our own lives, we fail to see any purpose or meaning for our existence. Life itself appears absent of any value. In addiction we live among the tombs of our own spiritual death.

Just as nobody could control or bind the demon-possessed man, nobody can control or cure an addict. The tearful pleas of family members have no effect. Friends try to reason it out of him. Bosses try to warn him, and they often fire him. Psychologists try to explain it out of him. Psychiatrists try to medicate it out of him. These efforts avail no lasting results. The addict is like the man who snapped chains and shackles as if they were string.

But the Lord of Love has the power we need to change. In the following paragraphs, I will look at the steps Jesus used to liberate the man from the evil power of Legion. We can apply the message of this story to any form of addiction or possession under which we may be suffering. As the man was cured of Legion, so we shall be cured of our personal demons.

When in the following description I employ the word addiction, I invite readers to understand any negative habit that plagues or troubles them.

1. Empty of Power

The very first thing we are shown by this story is that when trapped in addiction, we have as much power over our addiction as the man had over Legion—none at all. We can no more overcome our addiction by our own strength of will than the man possessed by Legion was able to cast the demons out of his body and mind by his own power. No amount of desire to do what is right and good can extract us from the grip of our personal Legion. It is vital we realize that when we are held by addiction, our very will has been hijacked. The first step toward freedom is to admit that we are powerless over the force of the addiction.

The word "empty" describes the situation of our spirits in relation to addiction. We have become empty through exhaustion. The gas tank is dry. We've spent all our energy and have no hope left. But the meaning goes deeper. We are also "empty" in a more fundamental way. All power belongs to God. He is the Potter and we the clay. We are mere vessels, empty of any strength or power. But as an empty vessel, we can receive, retain, and exercise God's power. We might even say that the fundamental quality that makes us human is that in and of ourselves we are empty. We are branches that must be attached to the vine. Being made in the image and likeness of God, our soul is of Love. But this is God's power within us, and not our own. Being empty allows us to receive God's life and love within us.

2. Misery

Just as important as admitting powerlessness is coming to realize the full extent of the damage in our lives and the lives of those around us caused by addiction. In the account, the man's life was truly a living hell. It was worse than death. He cut himself and lived among corpses. He moaned in anguish. He lived alone with no family or friends. When we are possessed by addiction, our lives are likewise a living hell. We damage ourselves and live amidst our own spiritual death and decay. Even when in the presence of others, we are isolated from them. We cannot make meaningful connections. Other people may fear to be close to us. We hurt those who draw near and try to help. We frustrate them. We make their efforts seem as worthless as the chains and shackles used in the attempt to control the possessed man. Until we see how lonely and dead our lives are because of the addictive possessing forces, we are probably not ready for healing.

Even if we suffer lesser addictions such as a criticizing spirit, or one of pessimism, or self-obsession, or desperation for attention, or obsession with work, or constant anger, we still find ourselves in misery. These subtle and seemingly slight forms of possession lead us to severe isolation. Our attitude causes others to distance themselves from us.

3. Petition Jesus for Help

After we admit to our powerlessness and to the misery of our lives, we are ready for an encounter with Jesus. When Jesus drew near to the place where the man dwelt, the man came running toward him, bowed down, and worshiped him. The possessed man knew his life was hell, and he knew that he needed help. God has the power to heal us from even the worst addictions. And he will do so—but first we need to ask.

We, like the man, need to worship Jesus and pray for mercy. Imploring the Lord for help enforces the conviction that we are, of ourselves, powerless. It proves at least some measure of desire for his healing. It also proves that we have at least a grain of faith in him. As Jesus says, even faith as small as a grain of mustard will grow until it moves the mountainous problems of addiction. Before Jesus will enter into our lives, we must invite him in. He will not force his healing on anyone. Worshiping and begging for help is the way to invite Jesus into our lives. It is the way to plant that mustard seed of faith within our hearts.

Notice what came out of the man's mouth immediately after he worshiped him: "What have you to do with me, Jesus, Son of the Most High God? I adjure you by God, do not torment me." This shows us that we need not have a perfect sense of separation from our possession in the beginning. Our desire for healing and love for our Savior may be mixed in with a great deal of resistance from the addictive force. The Lord of Love is merciful and doesn't require a perfect petition. Just contacting him in the midst of our confusion is enough for him to start helping us.

Legion spoke through the man's mouth: "Do not torment me!" When similarly possessed by addictive spirits, it seems as if God is at least in part responsible for our unhappy, tormented plight. We may wonder, "Why does God not help me? Why does God hate me?" In later stages, we will come to see that the Lord of Love is a torment only to the possessing spirits that are antagonistic to the ways of love. But until we have come to clearly delineate between the will of Love within us and the destructive spirits of the past that have come to possess us, encountering God may very well feel unpleasant. More important than the motive or content of what we say to the Lord at this point is the fact that we are willing to call out to him and contact him at all. All we have to do is start talking to God while on our knees.

4. Open and Expose

The next lesson we learn from this text is that we must open up and expose the addictive force for what it is. Jesus asks the demons their name. I am certain that Jesus knew the name of the demons; his motive in asking was to expose Legion to the light of truth. Addictions thrive by means of lies and deceit. Lies tell us that we are doing OK. Lies tell us that "just this one time" won't hurt. Lies tell us that the addiction is who we are and that we cannot change. The lies are varied, but they are all designed to keep us trapped.

By forcing the demons to name themselves, Jesus exposed them to the light and began to separate them out of the man. When Legion was forced to speak its name, the possessed man could see clearly that the spirits were separate from him. They lived in him, but they had a name different from his own. This was important for the man to hear, since he surely had trouble distinguishing his own consciousness from that of the demons. Without help from God, we cannot distinguish self from the possession and so remain entangled within its web. Jesus here invites us to see through the lies and to delineate our sense of self from the destructive will of the addiction. Having broken down the web of deceit surrounding Legion, Jesus already began freeing the man. Legion knew its time in the man was coming to an end.

We must learn to distinguish between the will of Legion and our sense of self. We can't delineate between the addiction and our sense of self without first bringing the truth about our addictive desires and behaviors to the light. Many of us spend a good deal of energy denying, minimizing, and excusing those aspects of our being that we know are unpleasant. It is very therapeutic to sit down and write down the truth about the desires and deeds that arise from the possessing force. We might start with these words: *The will of the legion of possessing spirits and the consequent deeds are as follows*...

This list should be a comprehensive and detailed account of the destructive habit. If we find that we fear taking this step, we likely don't believe that the addiction is derived from a force outside of ourselves. We don't yet see that we have been oppressed. If we seek to gloss over or hide the truth of our misdeeds and miscreant desires, we are actually helping to keep Legion lodged within us. Why would we seek to protect our tormentor unless we mistook the tormentor to be a part of our own being? It is not us. It is an alien, subjugating force.

Once we have exposed the here-and-now data of our personal Legion, we can go one step farther in exposing and separating Legion from our being. We can explore and write about the etiology of our personal Legion. Where did we learn this habit? What ancestors were similarly possessed and passed on the legacy of Legion? If we are alcoholic, for example, where did the alcoholic way of thinking and living arise from? A good therapist can wonderfully facilitate this process. When we come to see the contextual social and historical sources of our habits, it is much easier to understand the habits as external spirits or forces that have come to possess us. We are all born as innocent infants. Were we all given a perfect rearing in heaven, we'd not fail to become angels. On earth, however, the innocent child cannot help but be exposed to various less-than-loving and less-than-innocent stimuli. The innocent child that the Lord of Love created is held hostage by the spirit of these negative influences. These spirits animate us to action, and we come to misinterpret these spirits as ourselves.

The biggest lie lurking within all addiction is that the destructive, possessing desire is a fundamental part of who we are when in fact it is a foreign presence within us. If we can hold onto this idea even in the midst of temptation, we are moving closer to liberation.

The goal of this step is to undo this process—to peel back the layers until we see that the habits, addictions and possessing spirits are not our fundamental being, but invading malicious forces.

We can take Jesus's lead and call the destructive desires we feel by a name. When we feel tempted, we can say, "There's Legion again, trying to possess me, trying to pretend that it is me." By giving those addictive desires a name other than our own, we force a wedge between them and our sense of self. It may be helpful for us to come up with a name for the possessing spirits. If we are possessed by grumpy spirits, for example, we may wish to call it "The Grumpers." This distancing is an essential step in our recovery. Instead of thinking, "I want to drink, smoke, shoot up, gamble, lust, rage, and eat that whole cake," we think, "Legion wants me to screw my life up. But *I* want God's peace and joy."

Another lie that possessing spirits throw at us is that we can somehow learn to overpower and conquer our addictions on our own. In the story, Jesus also showed the man that he was possessed not by some single spirit, but by an entire society of beings that wished him harm. This surely helped the man understand why he was so very powerless. It is important to realize that when we struggle against possessing forces armed only with our own resources, we aren't on a fair playing field. We don't see it, but we are one against a legion of enemies. We cannot succeed by our own strength.

Finally, a powerful lie spun by the invaders is that we cannot change. We can hear someone say: *This is who I am—a grump. I cannot change.* Or another might say: *I'm too old to change. I've always had this gambling problem and I always will.* To see through these lies, we have to come to believe that in fact we can change. This can be hard after years of failure. However, with the Lord of Love, nothing is impossible.

In summary, this step entails uncovering the lies of the addictive force. There are four fundamental lies by which the possessing forces attempt to control us. The four lies are these:

1. I don't have a problem.
2. The addiction or habit is who I am.
3. I can overpower the addiction on my own.
4. I cannot change.

It is worth noting that the lies actually contradict each other. The first and second are polar and mutually exclusive extremes. The second two lies similarly contradict one another. This irrational juxtaposition proves that these ideas are indeed lies. Once convinced, we can focus on their opposite truths:

1. I do have a problem.
2. I am given over to problem spirits, but I am not the problem.
3. I am not on a level playing field; I need help.
4. With God's help, I can be set free and will change!

5. Widen the Gap

Judging one's self as evil and so trying to drown in self-hatred is counterproductive. The addict must learn to condemn and drown the addiction, while recalling that God loves us all. He created *all* of us in his image and as his children we *all* have a purpose in being alive. Legion drowns in the sea with the pigs. The man remains alive on the land with newly restored sanity. We must widen the gap between the addictive will and our sense of self.

Knowing its reign within the man was over, Legion begged Jesus to be sent into a new host, a herd of over two thousand pigs. It was a life-changing experience for this man to see his hateful tormentors of years annihilated in the sea. Jesus here shows us that the death of many pigs was worth the restoration of a single human being to sanity. The lives of two thousand swine is a small price to pay for the salvation of a man.

This has an allegorical meaning as well. Pigs wallow in their own feces and eat rubbish. We can see them as images of our lowest, self-serving desires. We all have animal instincts to self-preservation, to self-pleasure, and to self-aggrandizement. But we are more than these. We are wonderfully created with the capacity to grow in wisdom, humility, gratitude, and love—the things of spirit.

When the force of Legion begins to weigh upon us and powerfully urge us toward destructive acts, we are wise to recall that we are more than our selfish animal instincts. In the story, the power of Legion caused the pigs to drown while the man remained on the hill, now in his right mind. Our right mind is our spiritual mind.

To the extent we have come to identify with the qualities of our inner being—humility, gratitude, love for wisdom, concern for others, and a sense of unity—we can rest our minds atop this peak of insight and watch as self-serving desires drown themselves within their own insanity. When we are in touch with gratitude, cravings disappear. When we care about the well-being of others, we are not so concerned with serving the self. When we are humble, we don't feel entitled to self-indulgence. When we love wisdom, we dislike foolishness.

The trick is to remain focused on the things of spirit. We are children of Divine Love. We are not mere biology, nor are we maladjusted cultural influences.

We further widen the gap between our sense of self and the addictive, destructive desires by praying that they be removed from us and drowned, so to speak. In this way we have established a counter-will that gives contrast to the addictive will. This offers us a foothold against the destructive desires. Legion or addiction no longer has a monopoly on our thoughts or our will.

It also helps, while meditating, to imagine our addiction as pigs running into the sea and drowning. When we look at our internal struggle in this way, it gives us another step of distance from the will of the addiction. We might get on our knees and explain to Jesus, "Lord, I am willing to have my pig-like desires die that my human nature may be realized." We are making a choice. Jesus is beginning to restore the will and freedom that had been completely dominated by addiction, Legion.

6. End the Behaviors

We must end our addictive behaviors. There is simply no way to overcome addiction without pain and work. Inevitably, as addicts, we will at some point wish to indulge in the addiction. If we are to recover, we must at that moment make the decision to resist temptation and desist from the destructive behavior.

In the death of the pigs, Jesus openly displayed the immense and destructive power of Legion. Jesus simultaneously revealed his own might. Though the demons were exceedingly powerful, they were obedient and immediately succumbed to his will. They were no match at all for the Lord.

All of this, along with the preceding steps, helps us to end our destructive behaviors. We can recall that Jesus has the power needed to resist. Unless we believe that Jesus has the power to save us, we'll be trying to do it on our own strength and so will fail. But he saved the man from Legion, and he can save us from our personal Legion as well. We can also recall that the death of our selfish desires is worth the salvation of our humanity, our soul. As we call on Jesus's aid, we can remember he is infinite, endless love.

7. Recognize and Resist the Pig-Feeders

Not everyone was happy about the death of the pigs. Our next task is to see that after the external force has been separated from us, there is still a part of us, represented by the swineherds, that does not appreciate what is happening. They liked their pigs and the way things were. The herdsmen were unable to share in the man's incredible joy. They missed out on a real occasion to celebrate—the incurable man was cured! All they saw was that their pigs were dead. They feared economic loss; but they also feared the awesome power of Jesus and asked him to leave.

As we are increasingly liberated from the Legion of our old cravings and thoughts, we notice difficult feelings welling up within us, the feelings that the addictive patterns had been covering over—fear, guilt, resentment, unworthiness, self-loathing, depression, anger, and all the rest. These feelings are hard to deal with, so a part of us doesn't appreciate the sobriety and recovery that is taking place. These anti-sobriety sentiments are depicted by the herdsmen. These pig keepers were not concerned with the man, but with their own personal gain. They were mercenary.

The pigs represent self-indulgence. The herders represent worry, resentment, guilt, and other, similar tensions. These emotions profit from addictive self-indulgence (the pigs) because such indulgence temporarily mollifies these hard-to-deal-with feelings. These are the feelings that amplify our animal instincts. These feelings feed the pigs.

Once we refrain from self-indulgence, we are left with the underlying uncomfortable feelings. The story is not explicit about how to deal with these tensions. The absence of explanation is an answer of sorts. Just as the story does not focus on dealing with the swineherds but on the man's interaction with Jesus, so when these tensions arise, the best thing we can do is focus on our relationship with the Lord of Love. If we focus on worry when it arises, we only end up more worried. The same is true with guilt and frustration. *How can I be a more loving human being? How can I serve someone else? How can I show gratitude?* Asking these kinds of questions replaces the worry, guilt, and frustrated thoughts with positive thoughts and actions.

8. Entreat Jesus for Direction

As Jesus is climbing into the boat to leave, the healed man begs to come with him. When the swineherds of our heart throw up resistance to our growth in recovery, it's time to do as this man did—find Jesus. In the face of our internal resistance to recovery, we get on our knees and ask to be with Jesus. We tell Jesus that we wish to follow him and be with him. If we seek Jesus and seek his will for us, he will show us what to do. This step and the previous one are intimately bound together. When we feel the worries and tensions represented by the pig-feeders, it is a signal that it is time to get on our knees.

9. Declare Our Salvation

The man wanted to follow Jesus, but Jesus had a different plan for him—to proclaim to all his friends the glory and mercy of the Lord. After years of possession and life in the tombs, this man likely had no friends. But he declared his story throughout the city of Decapolis and "everyone was amazed." What a thrill it must have been for him to share his story and bring many people to faith in Jesus, the one who saved him.

An important step for us in letting God heal and liberate us from addiction is to share our story. We absolutely must communicate to other people what God is doing for us. We must explain to people what our lives were like while we were stuck in our addiction and how wonderful it is to be free at last. When in the midst of a temptation—be it large or mild—we reach out and connect with others. This act is proof that God is working a miracle in our lives. The fact that we contact another human being rather than indulging in our addictive desires is the miracle. In the past, we would not have been able to do this.

Because it is difficult to think clearly in the face of addictive desire, I've manipulated the words of each step heading to form an easily remembered word: "EMPOWERED."

E Empty of Power. We are empty vessels, exhausted of power.

M Misery. Life under the dictatorship of Legion is misery.

P Petition Jesus for Help. Through prayer, we open ourselves to receive the Lord's power.

O Open and Expose. We open up and expose the lies by which addiction keeps us subjugated. We come to see addiction as an alien force

W Widen the Gap. By focusing on the fact that we are spiritual beings, we widen our mental distance from the desires of the possessing force.

E End the Addictive Behaviors. We refuse to act on its impulses.

R Recognize and Resist the Pig-Feeders. When fears, resentments, and the like arise, we recognize them as mercenary foreigners to our spiritual lives.

E Entreat Jesus for Direction. We seek to be with the Lord and know his will.

D Declare our Salvation. We share the news of the Lord's salvation in our lives with others.

In times of temptation, we can stop and remember this word, "EMPOWERED." From there we can mentally recall each of these essential steps. Just taking time to review these steps will help break up the power of the temptations. Then, if we go through and do each of these steps, we will truly be empowered by God to overcome our addictions. The Lord will fill the empty vessel of our being with his strength and salvation. Anyone who is in recovery from an addiction knows that this recovery is nothing short of a major miracle. I believe this miracle is available to all who are interested.

Community is a key component of this miracle in multiple ways. In our individualistic culture, we tend to want to take care of things by ourselves, especially our internal struggles. However, if we consider the possible roots of this desire, we see that they are not healthy. We may be simply too embarrassed to admit our weaknesses to others. Yet if we really understand that our addictive thoughts and behaviors arise from forces outside of ourselves, then we will not feel embarrassed. On the contrary, we will feel indignant and want to blow the whistle on the oppressive spirits. Thus, if we allow feelings of embarrassment to block us from working within a healing community, we are still deluded and subjugated by the possessing spirits.

The other reason we may wish to achieve liberty from addiction by ourselves is that we believe we are more likely to succeed than when we work in concert with others. All I can say to this is that if I am oppressed by a legion of powerful foes, I want enlist as much help as I possibly can.

We need a safe community where we can talk about the abuses

we endured from the forces of addiction. We need to be able to talk about it, because the more we talk about addiction as an overwhelming and external force, the more we will awaken to the fact that it truly is just that. We are then empowered to escape its merciless rule. We also need community to fulfill the final command of Jesus within this healing—that we go and tell our friends. If he who saves us tells us to share the good news, it is extremely important that we do so. It is important for others to hear, and it is equally important for our own well-being. Communicating our story of addiction and salvation to others further sustains us in sobriety.

Though not identical, there are clear parallels between the message of this story and the methods of the twelve-step programs that continue to heal millions of people from a wide variety of addictions—admitting powerlessness and unmanageability; petitioning the Lord for help; exposing the addictive activities and desires to the light; making separation between the addiction and our sense of being; continuation in monitoring and resisting antirecovery sentiments; seeking contact with the Lord; sharing our healing/recovery with others. All of these elements are shared by both lists. When we include the steps and lessons gained in the first two chapters of this book—finding God, admitting our faults, making amends, and forgiving others—we arrive at a complete harmony.

If you suffer addiction, I recommend embracing a twelve-step program without hesitation. By participating in twelve-step recovery groups, we are exposed to the exhilarating salvation and power of the Lord at work in the lives of many men and women. We get front-row seats to the greatest show on earth—salvation. In recovery groups we are among people who truly understand our problems and with whom we can be completely honest without mistrust or reserve. An important lesson we've learned is that we must expose the truth about the addiction. A twelve-step meeting is a wonderful arena for this work.

When we are in the midst of our addiction, it is difficult for us to believe that Jesus can heal us. But the healed lives of millions of people in the recovery rooms prove that God heals people from even the most severe and desperate addictions. Addicts are often left with very few friends. They are emotionally shut down and their behaviors have isolated them. But in recovery circles we meet true friends. We meet people who hear our story and rejoice with us. Twelve-step recovery groups allow members to believe in any God.

Toward the end of the Gospel of John, before Jesus was crucified and rose from the grave, we read that he repeatedly promised to send the Helper, the Holy Spirit. I understand the Holy Spirit to be the powerful spirit of God as it works in and through human beings. So when we participate with others in hard spiritual labor, we can know that God is speaking to us by means of the men and women around us. When we work with others toward spiritual evolution, Jesus himself sits with us in the guise of other men and women. He says, "I am in the least of my brothers." For some, twelve-step programs may not be the way. Maybe we work with our spouse. Maybe we find our spiritual home in a prayer fellowship or within the group working through this book. Regardless, working with others is important and when we do so, God is present. "For where two or three are gathered in my name," says the Lord of Love, "I am there among them" (Matt. 18:20).

As is the case in many healings, this healing may not be a once-and-forever affair. We may need to go through the steps of this healing many times. Every time we sense the addiction trying to gain control of our actions, it is critical that we review this healing. We can receive this healing many times even in a single day.

It's truly wonderful that though it is the Lord healing us, we aren't simply passive recipients. The healing involves a lot of activity on our part. Yet action alone is not enough. Action within the context of faith is the combination that works. Love doesn't animate us like puppets. Rather, the Lord of Love invites us to participate in the dance of life.

Twelve Steps of Recovery

1. We admitted we were powerless over addiction—that our lives had become unmanageable.

2. Came to believe that a Power greater than ourselves could restore us to sanity.

3. Made a decision to turn our will and our lives over to the care of God as we understood him.

4. Made a searching and fearless moral inventory of ourselves.

5. Admitted to God, to ourselves, and to another human being the exact nature of our wrongs.

6. Were entirely ready to have God remove all these defects of character.

7. Humbly asked him to remove our shortcomings.

8. Made a list of all persons we had harmed, and became willing to make amends to them all.

9. Made direct amends to such people wherever possible, except when to do so would injure them or others.

10. Continued to take personal inventory and when we were wrong promptly admitted it.

11. Sought through prayer and meditation to improve our conscious contact with God as we understood him, praying only for knowledge of his will for us and the power to carry that out.

12. Having had a spiritual awakening as the result of these steps, we tried to carry this message to addicts, and to practice these principles in all our affairs.

Healing from Legion

1. Empty of Power. We are empty of power over that Legion, addiction. We are empty vessels.

2. Misery. Our addictive behaviors have brought our lives to misery (the man cut himself, moaned and lived among the tombs).

3. Petition Jesus for Help. Having observed our powerlessness and our misery, we petition the Lord for help (the man knelt before Jesus and worshiped).

4. Open and Expose. We expose the addictive desires and behaviors to the light (Legion speaks its name) and we delineate our sense of self from the addictive desires and behaviors (Legion leaves the man and enters the pigs).

5. Widen the Gap. We pray for the separation of sense of self from the Legion that plagues us.

6. End the Addictive Behaviors. We stop acting from the addictive desires (Legion drowns the pigs in the sea).

7. Recognize and Resist the Pig-Feeders. Confronted with continuing anti-recovery desires, we resist them as mercenary and foreign to our true best interests (the pig herders).

8. Entreat Jesus for Direction. We entreat Jesus that we be allowed to be with him and to know his will for us (the man sought to be with the Lord).

9. Declare our Salvation. We declare to others the good news of Jesus's salvation in our life (at Jesus's request, the man told all of Decapolis of Jesus's glory).

MEDITATION

After entering into a meditative state of mind, locate a habit over which you feel you have little or no control. Now enter into the experience of the man possessed by Legion. Imagine yourself among the tombs, breaking out of chains, cutting yourself and moaning day and night. Feel the agony and despair of this man. You sense the Lord approaching from behind and whirl around. You run toward him. Jesus commands the spirit to leave you. You bow down and from your mouth you hear these words: "What have you to do with me, Jesus, Son of the Most High God? I adjure you by God, do not torment me!"

Then Jesus asks, "What is your name?"

From your mouth you hear, "My name is Legion; for we are many." You hear the spirits using your voice to say that they want to enter into the pigs. Suddenly, you feel the evil and oppressive force of the habit you have selected rushing out of your being and you watch as the multitude of pigs runs down the hill. So great is the herd of pigs, it takes a several minutes for them all to drown in the sea. You are overcome by a feeling of peace and freedom. You notice your breath and you feel that you are finally yourself. The pig herders come and tell Jesus to leave.

You worship Jesus and ask to follow him. He gives you a mission: proclaim the miracle to all.

LEAVES

1. Habits and addictions are external forces that possess us.

2. The will of these possessing spirits enters into us as if it were our own will.

3. Their destructive will is not who we are.

4. Addictions survive by means of lies.

5. Addiction makes us miserable but lies to us that it will make us happy.

6. We are not the problem, but we do have a problem.

7. We cannot solve the problem on our own, but with the help of the Lord and other people, we can be healed.

8. Underneath the activities of addiction are unresolved feelings of guilt, anger, fear, resentment, and the like, which are represented by the pig herders.

FRUIT

When in the midst of temptation, we run through the EMPOW-ERED checklist mentally. If we deem ourselves as having a true addiction or unrelenting bad habit, during the week we make a comprehensive exploration of each point as follows:

E Empty of Power. We are empty vessels, exhausted of power. We write down the ways in which we have tried to stop but were unable to do so. We write down all those behaviors that prove our powerlessness.

M Misery. Life under the dictatorship of Legion is misery. We write down all the misery we have endured due to the addiction or habit.

P Petition Jesus for Help. By prayer, we open ourselves to receive the Lord's power. We get on our knees and pray for help for an extended period of time.

O Open and Expose. We open up and expose the lies by which addiction keeps us subjugated. We come to see addiction as an alien force. We write down all the lies that the addiction feeds us.

W Widen the Gap. By focusing on the fact that we are spiritual beings, we widen our mental distance from the desires of the possessing force. We write down all the qualities that we have been given from the Lord of Love. We write down all those qualities that we would like to embody as spiritual beings. We meditate on this as our true self, given to us from the Lord.

E End the Addictive Behaviors. We refuse to act on its impulses.

R Recognize and Resist the Pig-feeders. When fears, resentments, and the like arise, we recognize them as mercenary foreigners to our spiritual lives. We write down all the underlying upsets and fears that cause us to want to return to our addiction.

E Entreat Jesus for Direction. We seek to be with the Lord and know his will in prayer and meditation.

D Declare our Salvation. We share the news of the Lord's salvation in our lives with others. We share all the writing that we have done for the previous tasks with a trusted friend or mentor.

This is a lot of work to accomplish, yet I believe the rewards are worth it. If you are working through one chapter of this book per week, I recommend working on the task of just one letter from the word EMPOWERED each day. However, there are nine letters and, for those using this book in a group setting, only six days between group meetings. Fortunately, these meetings give us a chance to perform the final task—declare the way the Lord has worked in our lives over the previous week. This still leaves us with two extra tasks. One of these tasks is to "end the addictive behaviors." This can be done in conjunction with the step that follows, "recognize and resist the pig-feeders." The final remaining task is to "entreat Jesus for direction." This task can hopefully become a daily part of our prayer and meditation practices and a way of life. Alternatively, you may decide to spend more than one week on this chapter.

DISCUSSION QUESTIONS

1. Did you notice any positive shift this week in relation to this healing?

2. What was your experience of the meditation exercise? What was it like entering into a state of powerlessness?

3. If you feel comfortable communicating about the habit or addiction you chose to work on, and felt some relief from its grip as a result of this week's miracle, please share with the group.

4. In relation to which step(s) did you feel the most resistance?

5. Which of the steps was most useful?

6. What was it like to work on this healing and to share it with another?

7. Did you gain any insight into the lives of others who struggle with addiction? From this perspective, how did it feel to go through the meditation?

4

HEALING FROM INNER WARFARE

"Go in peace."

Mark 5:21–43

When Jesus had crossed again in the boat to the other side, a great crowd gathered around him; and he was by the sea. Then one of the leaders of the synagogue named Jairus came and, when he saw him, fell at his feet and begged him repeatedly, "My little daughter is at the point of death. Come and lay your hands on her, so that she may be made well, and live." So he went with him.

And a large crowd followed him and pressed in on him. Now there was a woman who had been suffering from hemorrhages for twelve years. She had endured much under many physicians, and had spent all that she had; and she was no better, but rather grew worse. She had heard about Jesus, and came up behind him in the crowd and touched his cloak, for she said, "If I but touch his clothes, I will be made well." Immediately her hemorrhage stopped; and she felt in her body that she was healed of her disease.

Immediately aware that power had gone forth from him, Jesus turned about in the crowd and said, "Who touched my clothes?" And his disciples said to him, "You see the crowd pressing in on you; how can you say, 'Who touched me?'" He looked all around to see who had done it. But the woman, knowing what had happened to her, came in fear and trembling, fell down before him, and told him the whole truth. He said to her, "Daughter, your faith has made you well; go in peace, and be healed of your disease."

While he was still speaking, some people came from the leader's house to say, "Your daughter is dead. Why trouble the teacher any further?"

But overhearing what they said, Jesus said to the leader of the synagogue, "Do not fear, only believe." He allowed no one to follow him except Peter, James, and John, the brother of James. When they came to the house of the leader of the synagogue, he saw a commotion, people weeping and wailing loudly. When he had entered, he said to them, "Why do you make a commotion and weep? The child is not dead, but sleeping." And they laughed at him.

Then he put them all outside, and took the child's father and mother and those who were with him, and went in where the child was. He took her by the hand and said to her, "Talitha cum," which means, "Little girl, get up!" And immediately the girl got up and began to walk about (she was twelve years of age). At this they were overcome with amazement. He strictly ordered that no one should know this, and told them to give her something to eat.

~~~⟆

These two healings—the woman healed of her flow of blood and the raising of Jairus's daughter—are united both in the literal sense and in the spiritual sense that applies to our personal evolution. The two healings are presented in the same way, one enclosed within the other, in Matthew, Mark, and Luke. There are also some intriguing points of connection between the two stories. Jairus's daughter was twelve years old—the same number of years that the woman had suffered a flow of blood. Twelve is also about the age when a girl typically first begins to menstruate, which was the woman's problematic issue.

In the woman's case, she had been seeking a private personal healing, but Jesus made the healing public. Jairus, on the other hand, had asked Jesus for help publicly, but Jesus resurrected his daughter in private with the instructions to keep the healing a secret. One healing is the inversion of the other.

In both healings, Jesus's authority and wisdom were questioned.

In the former, the disciples were incredulous that Jesus would ask who touched him in the midst of the pressing masses. In the latter miracle, the mourners openly ridiculed Jesus when he said that the girl was not dead but sleeping.

In Mark and Luke, these two healings immediately follow the casting out of Legion. In Matthew seventeen verses fall between the story of Legion and these two stories. And as will be explored later, these seventeen verses reiterate the hidden spiritual message of these two healings. Just as these three healings—the possessed man, the woman, and the girl—are united in the letter of the Bible, so are they bound in spirit of the Word. These stories deal with recovering from the trauma induced by having our will possessed by external malicious forces, which I propose is the true reality within all addictions and stubborn bad habits. The healing of the man from Legion teaches us the nuts-and-bolts procedure we must take to escape hell into the arms of our loving Father. These latter two stories offer us a deeper look into the spiritual and psychological dynamics that keep us entrapped within addictive cycles and how the Lord of Love can liberate us from those cycles. In this chapter, we will focus specifically on the story of the woman who touched Jesus in the crowd; we will explore the healing of Jairus's daughter in the next chapter.

In some spiritual traditions, the natural world is referred to as the womb of our spirit. Along these lines, Jesus speaks these words:

Very truly, I tell you, you will weep and mourn, but the world will rejoice; you will have pain, but your pain will turn into joy. When a woman is in labor, she has pain, because her hour has come. But when her child is born, she no longer remembers the anguish because of the joy of having brought a human being into the world. So you have pain now; but I will see you again, and your hearts will rejoice, and no one will take your joy from you. (John 16:20–22)

Jesus also speaks to Nicodemus about being born spiritually. Our experiences in the natural world are the nutrients from which our spirit grows stronger in love. Our natural body is the womb from which our spiritual consciousness can be born. In this story we read that a woman had a flow of blood. I think it safe to presume this issue of blood originated in her womb. The more she attempted to control and improve this bleeding, the worse it became. She spent all of her money on physicians until she had nothing left, and yet they only made the problem worse. After twelve years, she was financially, physically, and emotionally spent.

The spiritual message hidden within this vignette is that in some cases, even our most concerted efforts to rid ourselves of habits arising from the natural instincts of our physical body will not only fail, but will actually aggravate and worsen the problem. The more we war with ourselves, the more wounded and exhausted we become. In our traumatized and weakened state, we have fewer spiritual resources—hope, faith, humor, resilience—from which to live a love-based life. And yet, we dare not give up trying to fight our bad habits. Like the woman in the story, we are trapped in a vicious cycle. We cannot stop trying to get better, but our efforts worsen the situation.

This healing is about despair. It paradoxically heals us of the hope of being healed—at least in the way we had imagined. It is about accepting our imperfections and coming to understand them as integral parts of God's perfection.

In ancient Jewish culture, a woman's menstruation, even when normal and healthy, was considered unclean. But a woman's monthly flow of blood is a part of God's perfect plan. It is a necessary aspect of a woman's biology that allows her to hold within her womb a developing child and finally give birth. When considered in this light, menstruation is not unclean, but precious or even holy.

I see life on earth similarly—it may be uncomfortable and untidy, but it is necessary and even holy because of the purpose it serves— our spiritual birth. If everything in life always went the way we wanted it to go, we would never be challenged; we would never have the opportunity to develop spiritually. Only in the context of personal disappointments and fears do we have the opportunity to turn our lives over to a will higher than that of our own, the will of God. And just as ancient cultures pathologized menstruation, so we tend to erroneously pathologize the untidiness of life. Sometimes, those of us who pursue a spiritual life get confused about what that spiritual life primarily entails. We begin to demand of ourselves an unrealistic moral purity. Any imperfection of deed, word, or will gives rise to an escalated attack against our natural instincts. We become spiritual perfectionists.

The truth is that as humans being born into utter spiritual ignorance and within a biological body, we are not ever going to be able to be spiritually pure. In fact, if we think we are spiritually perfect, we are suffering from two spiritual diseases—delusion and arrogance. The goal is not perfection. The goal is love. Love is our true spirit. Love is the spiritual being—our true self—that is formed within the womb that is our biological body. It is not necessary to be perfect in order to be loving. On the contrary, were it not for our own imperfections and the imperfections of those around us, love would be impossible. Loving a perfect person who is always nice, gentle, loving, understanding, humorous, personable, charismatic, and endearing is too easy. It's so easy that it isn't even really love. When we continue to give of ourselves to others despite their warts and flaws, then love is becoming something real.

We need our own flaws, too. Our weaknesses and imperfections keep us humble. They make us human. They soften us up and force us to give up sitting in the seat of judgment. To the extent we judge others for their faults, we are not loving them. Our own weaknesses and frailties wake us up to a spirit of mercy and gentleness with others who are similarly human. We use the word *human* to mean weak, and I think there is wisdom in this—"he's only human." To be human is to be weak. To accept this fact gracefully is to become humane.

Failure to accept imperfections in one's self leads to the spiritual equivalent of a pathological flow of blood. In expending all our effort toward becoming morally perfect, we only make matters worse, because we are still self-obsessed. We are so self-obsessed that we can't stand facing up to the fact that we have some flaws, that we are human. In other words, we can't stand not being God. I am not sure if there is any moral imperfection greater than insisting that the self should or could be God. Thus, again, the more we work toward this end, the more spiritually sick we become. Our spiritual vitality drains out of us, like the blood did from this poor woman. Though we don't usually consider addiction and bad habits as motivated and sustained by our effort to overcome addiction, I believe that at least in some cases it is true: *addiction is sustained by the attempt to overcome the addictive behaviors from a self-serving motive that appears to be a spiritual motive.*

We can imagine how the woman's flow of blood not only drained her physically, but mentally too. We can be sure that most of her thoughts and emotions were absorbed by this constant, distressing ailment and her search for a way to cure it. Her flow of blood would have become a part of the way she conceived of herself. Eventually the woman must have despaired of ever being cured save a miracle. When she heard the report of Jesus's powers to heal, she had to go. Yet she didn't want to make a public scene. She wanted a private, secret healing. She didn't want to admit that she was sick, especially not such a shameful kind of sickness. Though in modern culture we no longer consider menstruation "unclean," most of us do have some sense of shame or embarrassment about our reproductive organs. Given the option, most of us too would likely opt for a secret healing over a public one if our genitals were the location of our disease.

Jesus, though, had other plans. "Who touched my clothes?" he said. Jesus wasn't going to let her walk away without drawing the attention of this huge crowd to her ailment and healing. I have no doubt that Jesus already knew who touched him and what was wrong with her. He knew that Peter would catch a fish with enough money to pay the tax. He knew when and how he would die. He knew who he had healed. But the healing wasn't finished yet. He still needed to heal this woman of the spiritual and psychological illness that paralleled her physical illness.

Like the woman in the healing explored in chapter one, this woman faced stigmas and cultural oppressions. She was a woman, she was ill—a sign of sinfulness in that culture—and moreover, the nature of her illness would have brought her all the more stigma and shame. How humiliating it must have been for her to have all those doctors investigating and attempting their cures. But at least those encounters did not involve a large number of people. Now the truth was being exposed before a huge crowd. We read that "the woman, knowing what had happened to her, came in fear and trembling, fell down before him, and told him the whole truth." This was such an ordeal for her that she was actually trembling.

We have to ask ourselves, why would Jesus force such an ordeal onto her? I can come up with two reasons. The second (I'll get to the first later) is so that he can publically praise and affirm her. He calls her daughter and states that it is her faith that made her well. By honoring her in public, he contradicted and nullified her feelings of shame. I name this as the second reason because I don't believe it is the primary reason. As I see it, the first and most important reason Jesus confronted her in public is to break her pride—and, vicariously, our pride as well.

When we insist on being spiritually perfect or morally pure, the root problem is unhealthy pride in ourselves. We're trying to play God. What we think is a terrible flaw against which we unleash our full-on attack is really God's saving grace. When we are in such a state, the flaw is the only thing preventing us from becoming utterly and despicably conceited. We rage against our imperfection until we are broken. In this way, God breaks our pride. In the end we are no longer able to hide from the fact that we are deeply flawed. Addiction and stubborn habits are one of God's more painful and obtuse, yet effective, ways of healing us of pride.

As mentioned above, in both Mark and Luke, this healing follows immediately after the casting out of Legion. In Matthew there are just seventeen verses between the casting out of Legion and the healings of the woman and the girl. It is no coincidence that all the stories included within those seventeen verses involve Jesus associating with or forgiving sinners while the prideful Pharisees frown. First, he forgives the paralytic, and the Pharisees disapprove. Then Jesus takes a hated tax-collector as one of his disciples. This is immediately followed by the Pharisees griping as Jesus enjoys a dinner with sinners and tax collectors. The final few of those seventeen versus begin with John the Baptist's disciples questioning why Jesus's followers don't fast.

Part of Jesus's explanation is that "No one sews a piece of unshrunk cloth on an old cloak, for the patch pulls away from the cloak, and a worse tear is made. Neither is new wine put in old wineskins; otherwise, the skins burst, and the wine is destroyed; but new wine is put into fresh wineskins, and so both are preserved" (Matt. 9:16–17).

This teaching is traditionally explained as meaning the new ideas of Christ must be put into new, flexible minds. Aged wine is generally considered superior to new wine. Would Christ be calling his doctrine inferior to the old? Also, his example about wineskins follows immediately after one about repairing clothes, in which the Lord says that old clothes must be repaired with a similarly old patch. This doesn't align with the idea that these verses are talking about putting Jesus's new ideas into young minds at all. The point here is that the old is more serviceable than the new.

Thus an alternative way of understanding this parable is that our flaws are used for good by God. A new pair of pants does not need a patch. Only an old pair does; and it must be patched with a similarly old cloth. Only after we've been around the spiritual block a few times and come to recognize our weaknesses are we of much use to others who are in need. If we believe ourselves to be spiritually "new"—that is, near perfect—our attempts to help others, to patch them up, will only worsen the situation. A young spirit who hasn't yet been humbled by imperfections will judge, and the judgment will only make the spiritual tear of the other party worse. The wise humility acquired with age allows us to help others effectively.

The old wineskins that hold the old wine are not as flexible as the new, and so are inferior. Admitting our spiritual inferiority allows us to hold a better wine, that is, to be a more loving person. And if we are a new wineskin—i.e., we have no obvious problems—we will be filled with the new, inferior wine. When we don't recognize our inherent spiritual infirmity, we simply can't be very humble, and in the absence of seasoned humility, we won't be very loving. But every new wineskin eventually becomes old, and the wine within likewise becomes superior. So too, just by living life, humility is forced upon us.

So though it initially seems unkind, Jesus breaks the woman's pride, and ours, out of love. He knows we wish to evolve spiritually and he knows this is the only way. Love forces us to cry out in despair, "Yes, I'm flawed, and despite all my efforts, I am more flawed than ever." Ironically, when we despair of overcoming our problems by our own efforts, we are close to being healed.

We had been attempting to reign in, cage, and control our less savory aspects with our imagined self-power and pride. We were suffering under the delusion that we had spiritual motives and were attempting to control ourselves from spirituality. In truth, to the extent that pride, self-will, or imagined self-power were involved, we were still operating from our lower biological self and not from spiritual motives of love.

A story from Genesis offers the same message as this healing. Jacob, having been sent away from home to seek a wife, slaves away for his uncle Laban. Laban means *white*, a color associated with purity. Jacob is hoping to marry Rachel, whose name means *ewe*, a symbol for innocence and fertility, but instead he is given Leah, whose name means *weakness*. The symbolism is blatant, and it tells the same story as this healing miracle: slaving away for perfection and the hope of being innocent leads us to see our weaknesses.

Finally, Jacob gives up trying to please Laban and leaves with Rachel, Leah, and a group of kinsfolk. Rachel has stolen Laban's idols, and so Laban comes chasing after Jacob to get back his gods. Rachel hides them under her saddle and pretends to be menstruating and therefore unclean. Laban won't search where there is impurity. Besides, for a menstruating woman to sit on an idol would be an abomination in that culture; her father would never imagine she would do such a thing. In this story, Laban represents our prideful perfectionism. The idol of such an attitude is obviously perfection itself. The symbolic message is that purity and perfection, represented by the idols, don't exist as we imagine—a kind of squeaky-clean whiteness within the mess of life. In other words, God's perfect plan actually exists within the imperfection of our lives as human beings. Just as Laban can't find the idols, so our pride can't see perfection within messy life. Like the womb, life is sometimes uncomfortable and annoying, but it is a part of God's perfect and creative plan.

As the group continues on their way, Jacob wrestles God and, coming out on top, demands a blessing from God. The blessing is twofold. First, a new name, Israel, which among other things means *May-God-Persevere*. May-God-Persevere is a prayer that expresses humility. We aren't depending on our own might. God has indeed persevered—it is God who gives us humility. Another meaning of Israel is *He-will-rule-as-God*. How does God rule? With pure mercy and forgiveness. Ironically, we rule as God only after we stop trying to rule over our own lives. We judge as God judges (with pure forgiveness and mercy) only after we stop judging. God's perfection is within imperfections. Impurity and flaws are not a problem for Love. Before Jacob receives God's blessing, during the fight, God shrinks Jacob's loin muscle, which causes Jacob to limp the rest of his life. This symbolizes the same message: imperfection is a part of life and is, in fact, a blessing from God.

The message of the Jacob story is the same as the miracle involving the woman with the flow of blood. The miracle ends with Jesus's loving words: "Daughter, your faith has made you well; go in peace, and be healed of your disease." Again, faith is crucial; and again it is crucial that we well understand what faith in Jesus means. It means placing the well-being of all over and above our own desires.

I believe that much of our desire to be perfect is based in a desire to look good to other people. Our efforts are based in pride and love for our reputation. When we are engaged in the effort of extracting approval from others, we reduce people to servants in our mind. We make them agents in our efforts to soothe our own sense of self. No matter how generously we give of ourselves to them, we aren't actually loving them. We are simply loving ourselves by means of them. This pseudo-care is often referred to as "people-pleasing."

We are invited by this miracle to move beyond our concerns about what others think of us. The woman believed Jesus could heal her, and he did, but not in the discreet way she had hoped. We may believe Jesus can heal us of our problems, and he can, but often not in the discreet way we likely hope for. Jesus wants to heal us in the context of community. He wants to heal us in partnership with other human beings. He wants this for at least five reasons: one, to bless us with meaningful relationships based in mutual development and healing; two, to catalyze the healing of those around us by means of our healing; three, to catalyze our own healing by means of others; four, to remind us that God doesn't live in our heads or in a book alone, but in the "least" of us, that is, all of us; and five, to liberate us from worry about what others think about us.

Jesus didn't want this woman sneaking away healed in body, but still diseased in attitude. He demanded that the woman face her fear and shame and come forward before the masses with the truth. After the woman told all to Jesus in front of the large crowd, Jesus blessed her.

The woman left with a new freedom. The crowd she had feared because of her shame now held no power over her because of Jesus's public display of honor and affection. He called her "daughter." He said that her faith was such that it healed her. He blessed her with peace. But the point isn't that the crowd she had feared now respected her. The point is that it doesn't matter what the crowd thought one way or another.

Interestingly, an issue relating to this healing came up in my life just as I was editing this chapter. My parents came to Nepal, where I have lived for the past twelve years, for a visit. After about a week of lovely reunion, I noticed feelings of anger and resentment building up. Only after I stopped and purposefully thought about the reason for these feelings did I become aware of their origin. My nuclear family was in a crisis relating to one of our kids during my parents' visit. I was in an irritable mood. The feelings of anger in relation to my parents came from my sense of pride and concern for reputation. Though my parents had said nothing judgmental to me, I was upset that my parents were seeing me in an irritable mood and not at my spiritual best. My deluded ego had turned living a life of love into some kind of competition. When I felt I was "losing" the game of spiritual perfectionism, I got resentful and sullen. This is so ridiculous that I am smiling as I write this, and yet this truly was my state of mind. The source of the anger was pride.

Just as the doctors in this story made things worse with their efforts to heal her, so my pride makes things worse in its efforts to make me a better human. I wanted to be seen as spiritually fit and grew upset when I could not hold up this pretense. I then grew angry at myself for being angry. Thus when my effort to be spiritually fit was motivated by pride, I became less and less fit. I was becoming steadily more irrational, irritable, and angry. After I sat down and discovered where the feelings of resentment were coming from, I had the opportunity to admit to myself the truth: "I'm an imperfect human being with issues."

As soon as I simply accepted my imperfection, I no longer cared what others thought about me, and the feelings of resentment evaporated. And here in this book is my opportunity to be honest before others about one of my many weaknesses.

Perfectionism and love of reputation are ultimately not conducive to spiritual growth. To continue the journey, we must travel beyond fear- and self-based motives. When we share the truth of our imperfections with others two benefits occur. First, we are able to move beyond pride. Second, others around us may find comfort or encouragement by what we share. I certainly have gained much from the bravery of others who have been willing to share with me the truth about their life struggles.

Like the woman, we need to come into contact with our living Lord of Love. He lives in the community of humanity. Like the woman, we are blessed when we allow ourselves to be vulnerable by sharing our weaknesses and concerns with others. In this way we get real with ourselves and with others. This may take the form of sharing in a spiritual growth group. It may take the form of a first step in a twelve-step meeting. It may simply be a new, softer way of interacting with our loved ones. Rather than always problem solving, we may simply say, "Yeah, I know what you mean. Sometimes I really struggle with anger, too." We are now serving as a patch for an old pair of pants. We have some aged wine to offer others. It is hard to break through the fear of admitting our weaknesses to others. It is our faith in the Lord of Love that can motivate us to do so. Once we see that our old way is ineffective and based in selfishness, then we may find ourselves willing to try something new. We may be willing to try a more loving way of interacting both with others and with ourselves.

About five years ago, I had a vision that is apropos and that I'd like to share here. One of my spiritual weaknesses is perfectionism. At around the time of the vision, I had been struggling with all my might to improve myself, but, like the woman of this healing, the more I tried, the worse things seemed to be getting. I finally arrived at a state of utter despair. I felt angry at God for not helping me more, for leaving me in such a pitiful state. I went to bed and all night long I felt as if two forces were wrestling against one another in my mind. They were ascending as they wrestled, which is to say, the wrestling was carrying me farther away from perception of my body and physical surroundings. This wrestling lasted many hours, during which I could not sleep. Finally, I began to have a vision. On my left, lying face down in mud, was a woman in red. On my right was God. I could not see him, but could tell that he was there. I was standing on a plateau.

"Am I done?" I asked, hoping the struggle was over.

"No," was the reply that came from the Lord on my right.

"Why not?"

"You have to go back and help her." I knew he meant the woman, and I understood she represented my marriage and the life of humanity on earth.

"What's wrong with her?"

"She needs to be loved."

And then the Lord said something that has changed my life and that I will never forget. He said, "It is better to love imperfection with imperfect love than to love perfection with perfect love."

The vision ended at this point. It was just after four in the morning, and the first light of dawn was beginning to illuminate the world outside. I went out and greeted the morning. For two hours I sat and watched the world unfold around me. I have never felt such peace and gratitude as I felt for those few hours following the vision.

For me, the message of the vision is the same as the message of this story and of the Jacob story. Adoring perfect God with perfect adoration isn't the point of life. The point is that we love one another. And in loving one another, we will be faced with imperfections—our own and those of others. Yet this messy process is superior to the sterile adoration of a perfectly imagined idol.

I had been demanding more perfection from myself. That demand for perfection was making my life even more hellish. God was telling me that my imperfect attempts to love imperfect people were good enough. He didn't want or expect spiritual perfection from me or anyone else.

Somehow, bringing our problems to light develops compassion within us. It is as if for the first time we admit to ourselves, "I'm a human being with problems." We learn to accept our imperfection, and that simultaneously opens the door for us to accept other people despite their problems. We are liberated to see other people as people rather than means to soothe the ego. We begin to know and feel love. We begin to act with genuine compassion. When we are with others, we are freed to give rather than seek what we can get.

God blesses us in the presence of others. And in this public blessing, we not only regain our confidence and spiritual vitality, we also encourage others to share similarly. The blessing passes from one to another. Honesty is contagious. Others become willing to bring their truths of experience to Jesus's healing. They learn to overcome the false idol of the opinions of other people.

Jesus used the affliction of this woman to bring about God's kingdom in several ways. First, he healed her physically. Second, he revealed to many witnesses the glory of God's healing power within the context of her disease. Third, he released this woman from the tyranny of worry about the opinions of others. He freed her from the false idol of pride in reputation. Jesus also showed the surrounding crowd that it is better to be honest than to hide away our problems for fear of shame. And finally, Jesus offers us the same spiritual healing: we don't need to judge ourselves based on what others think or feel about us. God alone is our judge.

All of us are born into the prison of self. God's remedy involves sharing honestly with other people. And in this way, he dispels useless, prideful shame and fear.

The story about Legion reveals the steps to take in order to be liberated from addiction. This healing of the woman explains to us why and how to carry out the last of these steps, which is embodied in the word *declare*. We declare the truth about what our life was like and how the Lord is healing us. This story is an invitation card from God to enter fully and unreservedly into faith in his love for us. If we accept, he will put an end to the disease that drains us of all hope, joy, love, and strength. He will restore to us our spiritual lifeblood. He will fill us up with life, strength, and freedom.

After her encounter with Jesus, the woman gained a new sense of self-respect. She learned to stand tall and without shame in society. She gained a new, honest, and personal relationship with the living God. She regained her strength, sense of wholeness, and well-being. So it is with us. In sharing our story under God's guidance, we regain our self-respect. We regain the ability to stand tall and comfortable within society. We regain an honest and true relationship with God—no more trying to steal a miracle from behind. And we regain the spiritual strength and freedom needed to turn away, one day at a time, from our disease. Our sense of integrity has been restored.

In this miracle of the woman with the flow of blood, Jesus wants to heal us too. When accepted spiritually, the Lord's healing of the woman from her flow of blood initiates our healing from perfectionism. By this story he liberates us from enslavement to pride and the opinions of others, and also liberates us from our constant warring with ourselves. This healing occurs when, out of faith in the supremacy of Love, the inmost nature of our Lord, we surrender to the fact that we will always be imperfect and we allow ourselves to be humble and honest about our faults in the presence of others. When we do this our constant, draining war against our own being comes to an end and we receive a great sense of peace and relief. We can almost hear Jesus saying to us, "Go in peace."

MEDITATION

After entering into a meditative state, locate an issue in your life with which you have struggled, but in struggling, things only seem to get worse. Allow yourself to despair of your efforts. Now walk through this story as vividly as possible. You see a large crowd and know Jesus is in the midst. You decide to touch the border of Jesus's robe. You press through the crowd. You know that with your flow of blood, you are considered unclean and are not supposed to touch anyone. You wish to keep everything secret. Finally, you see Jesus and touch the hem of his garment. Suddenly you hear him say, "Who touched my clothes?" You begin to tremble. You hear his disciples questioning his words. But he keeps looking, and you know that he knows. You cannot control yourself as you fall down on your knees, shaking and weeping. You tell Jesus the whole story about your painful struggle to be well. Let it sink down into your heart as Jesus says to you, "Child, your faith has made you well; go in peace, and be healed of your disease."

LEAVES

1. Moral and spiritual perfectionism is based in pride and is an issue over which we need healing.

2. When motivated by self and pride, the more we try to improve, the more ill we become.

3. Life is messy. God's perfect plan exists within the imperfections of self and others.

4. Loving, not purity, is the goal.

5. The praise and approval of others is a false idol, not worth pursuing.

6. Shame is not helpful in our spiritual development.

7. When shame or desire for praise motivate us, we are sapped of true spiritual motivation and lifeblood.

8. It is important to be honest about our weaknesses with others.

9. Admitting our weaknesses and imperfections to other people heals us of perfectionism and also helps heal others of the same issue.

FRUIT

1. Allow yourself to be imperfect and weak.

2. Talk about your imperfection and weakness to a trusted friend or group.

3. Surrender in prayer the prideful effort to be perfect.

4. Focus and meditate on the fact that God's perfection exists within the imperfection of life on earth.

DISCUSSION QUESTIONS

1. What about this miracle story affected you?

2. Did you notice any positive change during the week?

3. What are the personal flaws you chose to focus on?

4. How did it feel to share your story with others?

5. Can you think of a time when your pride caused problems, or kept you from resolving one?

6. Were you able to trust and rest in God's perfection despite the imperfections of life on earth?

5

HEALING FROM LOST INNOCENCE

"Do not fear, only believe."

Mark 5:35–43

While he was still speaking, some people came from the leader's house to say, "Your daughter is dead. Why trouble the teacher any further?"

But overhearing what they said, Jesus said to the leader of the synagogue, "Do not fear, only believe." He allowed no one to follow him except Peter, James, and John, the brother of James. When they came to the house of the leader of the synagogue, he saw a commotion, people weeping and wailing loudly. When he had entered, he said to them, "Why do you make a commotion and weep? The child is not dead, but sleeping." And they laughed at him.

Then he put them all outside, and took the child's father and mother and those who were with him, and went in where the child was. He took her by the hand and said to her, "Talitha cum," which means, "Little girl, get up!" And immediately the girl got up and began to walk about (she was twelve years of age). At this they were overcome with amazement. He strictly ordered that no one should know this, and told them to give her something to eat.

In the last chapter, we discussed the miracle preceding this one, in which Jesus healed a woman with a chronic hemorrhage. We turn now to the raising of Jairus's daughter, the third and final healing in this cluster dealing specifically with how Jesus opens the way for us to overcome destructive habits and addictions. The news of the girl's death came while Jesus was still speaking to the woman with a flow of blood, saying, "Daughter, your faith has made you well; go in peace, and be healed of your disease." The healing of one daughter coincides with the death of another. On a symbolic level, I would even say that the healing of one actually precipitates the death of the other.

The healing of the woman with the flow of blood taught us to accept our imperfections. Acceptance that we are flawed and unable to become pure by our own strength ushers into our lives much-needed peace, but it also brings about a great sense of loss. One of the reasons we had been fighting so hard against ourselves was to prevent the total death of our innocence. We are now admitting our utter defeat. Just as Jairus realized his daughter was dead the moment the woman with the hemorrhage was healed, once we stop warring against ourselves, we become convinced that our innocence is irreversibly lost. Our hope and innocence, we admit, are dead. Like Jairus, we have no choice but to hope that somehow by coming to these meetings and sharing the truth before others, we will be restored to life. Picture a ragged Allied battalion in World War II coming out in the morning with hands up and white flags flying. They are convinced that they have lost the battle. What they don't realize is that during the night, Germany accepted defeat—the war is over, and there is no enemy on the other side of the field.

Children are wonderful. Their young eyes see the world with fresh wonder as alive and new. They are full of excitement and curiosity. They are not calloused. They are not self-conscious. They generally don't fret. They don't long harbor grudges. They are liberal and unreserved in their affection and emotions. They do not try to maintain pretenses; nor are they deceitful or cunning. They take joy in simple things that many adults overlook. Children radiate innocence. And to spend time with children is an opportunity for older, more callous hearts to see and appreciate the world afresh.

Jesus tells us that we must become like little children to enter the kingdom of heaven within. It is a state of mind filled with the simple joy of nonjudgmental appreciation, gratitude, and acceptance. Most of us, somewhere along the journey to adulthood, lose our ability to enjoy each moment for what it is, a wondrous miracle. We get wounded and scarred. We become fearful of life. Afraid to engage with life and others with love, we substitute care and appreciation with self-promoting ambitions and self-serving desires. We get bogged down in self-pity. We lose our ability to sense the grace and heaven that exists all around us.

One of the tragedies that many of us face as adults is the total loss of any sense of innocence. With this loss of innocence comes an inability to sense anything heavenly within us, or therefore around us, at all. We think that we have stepped outside the boundary of God's love. Like Jairus's servants, we wonder, "Why trouble the teacher?" Life becomes dreadful. We see the death of the hopeful, wonder-filled child we had once been. At this point, we know that our innocence is dead and that without a doubt we have arrived in hell. It is a devastating realization. And we are, of course, correct. This state of mind is nothing less than hell. We feel a devastation similar to what Jairus felt when he learned that his only daughter, once so vibrant and innocent, was dead. In our case, it is the innocence of our spirit that has died.

When drowning in this nightmare state of mind, all we can see is futility. This loss of hope perpetuates our bad habits and addictions. When life is already miserable and we feel there is no chance for improvement, we have very little motivation to change.

But this lack of hope is part of the necessary process of our healing. To recover from this state of mind, we have to first lose hope and hit rock bottom. The rock we find is the cold, hard truth that in and of ourselves, we are hopeless, powerless, without innocence, and in hell. But God calls himself the rock, and this hard, stony truth is a blessing in disguise. It is what we need to learn to move forward and access God's mercy, love, and innocence.

We can imagine the desperation Jairus feels as his daughter lies at the point of death. As the leader of a synagogue, he faces a great deal of criticism and disdain from Pharisees, scribes, and other synagogue leaders for turning to Jesus for help. But obviously, things such as social norms and reputation have become trivial in the face of his great love for his only daughter and his hope to save her life. Perhaps in similar desperation, we have tried everything to retain innocence within our lives. Typically, only after every other effort has failed are we willing to lay down our pride and throw our lives down at the feet of the Lord of Love and admit our desperate situation.

The name Jairus means *enlightener*. When desperation forces us to a place of humility similar to that of Jairus, we are on the verge of becoming enlightened. Before arriving at Jairus's house, Jesus heals the woman with a flow of blood. Symbolically, like Jairus, we come to Jesus in the desperate hope that his way of love can restore us to innocence. The Lord's initial answer, expressed within his healing of the woman, is that imperfection is a part of life. It is our pride and love of reputation that causes us to war against our imperfection in the hope of obtaining innocence. In other words, innocence is not the same thing as purity and perfection.

Innocence is trusting the Lord, no matter what goes on. This is Jesus's second lesson to Jairus. After the servants report that Jairus's daughter is dead, Jesus commands him to believe. Jairus has to trust in Jesus despite the apparent hopelessness of the situation. In this scene, Jesus is shifting our understanding of what innocence means. Innocence in terms of purity and perfection is dead, and always has been. Trusting the Lord no matter what is going on is true innocence.

Even while Jesus is still speaking to the woman whom he healed of the flow of blood, servants from Jairus's house come and tell him he no longer need "trouble" Jesus—his little girl has died. Jairus is utterly devastated. I imagine that a numbness accompanied by desperate denial must have overcome his consciousness: *This can't be happening. This can't be true!* If we allow the spirit of this story to enter into us, we may be entering a similar state of shock, despite the peace we feel in knowing we no longer need war against ourselves. We are shocked by the realization that the innocence we had so hoped for and for which we had so mightily fought is nonexistent. Our hope for innocence, as we understood it, is dead.

Blessedly, hopelessness is quickly followed by hope. Jesus bolsters Jairus's spirit (and so ours), saying, "Do not fear, only believe." Jairus may not be able to muster much genuine faith, but his desperate love for his daughter makes him cling to this last hope. He really has no choice but to hope. This willingness to hope, despite our better judgment, is the beginning of the revival of the girl representing our innocence. The shift has occurred. Before, we thought of innocence as purity and perfection, and we fought fiercely for it. Finally, we realized that we had failed. We weren't able to be perfect or pure. We had to lose hope in this kind of innocence before we were able to be given true innocence from the Lord—willingness to trust in him regardless of what life throws at us and regardless of our perception of the gravity of our situation.

Arriving at Jairus's house, Jesus says the young girl is not dead but asleep. The crowd of weepers gathered around scorns him. The voices of these mourners are within us. When we despair of our ability to be the person we wish to be, we can't help but ridicule the idea that our innocence is still alive. "No," we say, "I know for sure: I am spiritually dead." Scorn is an unavoidable symptom when innocence has died. Within the scorn lie the last vestiges of pride. What would have motivated the weepers to ridicule Jesus except pride? Had they been motivated by love, they would have at least held their tongues, and they may have even hoped for the best.

The weepers reveled in being right and making sure Jesus understood that he was wrong. As human beings, we like to be right.

Being right makes us feel powerful and superior to others. It is the delusion of pride that causes us to cling to an "I'm a hopeless case" mentality. By saying *nobody can heal me, not even Jesus,* our pride maintains its last hold on our lives. We can be right in our wrongness. We can be powerful by predicting our personal damnation. We gain a sense of security and self-control by predicting our inability to be controlled or saved.

The other side of this scornful coin is self-pity. *Oh I'm so screwed up! I am such a mess! I'll never know happiness.* Sentiments of self-pity are our inner professional mourners. We love to go at it and bemoan our wretchedness! Self-pity is pride in disguise because through self-pity we maintain a sense of power and safety in our lives. If we condemn ourselves first, nobody's opinion has the power to harm us. In severe cases, we even sabotage others' attempts to help us so as to prove ourselves right and thus maintain our power—*I knew I was hopeless.* In professional psychology circles, people exhibiting such behaviors are known as *complainer-rejecters,* and they are considered among the most difficult to help, for obvious reasons. By wallowing in self-pity, we retain power over our emotions and our actions. We are miserable and unsavable by an unconscious choice. We are willing to sacrifice potential happiness for the sake of feeling like we are in control.

So if Jairus's willingness to trust and follow the Lord is the beginning of the girl's resurrection, the ejection of the professional mourners is the next step. The resurrection of hope and innocence is furthered when the Lord of Love forces our self-pity and our scoffing out of our consciousness. He does this in relation to our faith that his ways of love can indeed heal us. To the extent we allow this hope into our hearts and minds, the scorn and self-pity are ousted. Hope excludes scorn and self-pity. It was necessary to lose all hope in ourselves so that Jesus could fill us with hope in his love.

The Lord never acknowledged that the girl was dead. In his view of things, the innocence within us has never died. Paradoxically, for innocence to live within us, we must come to believe it has died.

Accepting that on our own we are unable to sustain the life of innocence is in fact an act of innocence. It is innocent because we are admitting our powerlessness and humble need for God's mercy. The girl had to die to humankind before she could live to God.

Jesus permits only Peter, James, John, and the parents to remain with him and the girl. He resurrects her with his tender touch and the words, *"Talitha cum"*—"Little girl, get up!" We can only imagine the pure elation and overwhelming joy that engulfed the parents. Their daughter was alive! She had died; all hope was lost. Yet in the presence of his touch and his words, she was now alive and walking.

The same is true with us. After we see the deadness of our own self, Jesus now has the chance to give us real life, his life. We now know that we are alive only because the Lord Jesus loves us and has mercy on us. We now know that without Jesus, we are nothing; we are dead. We are now ready and eager to accept his life-giving touch and hear his enlivening words.

That small group assembled around Jesus in the room represents the part of us that can't let go of the hope that somehow the Lord of Love might heal us to innocence. Jairus clung with hope to Jesus's words, "Do not fear, only believe." The stakes were too high to give up. Our innocence is actually held within the Lord, and so cannot be utterly destroyed. He never gives up on us.

Jesus sent the scoffers away and didn't let anyone into the house accept a very select few. The parents were instructed to do three things: "Believe," "Give her something to eat," and "Tell no one." To regain our sense of innocence, the first thing we must do is believe that the Lord of Love is in charge and guiding our lives, regardless of how hopeless we feel. In him, we can become as little children and so enter the kingdom of heaven.

Jesus commanded the parents to feed the little girl. We must nurture our innocence. We engage in activities that foster our innocence—a walk in the woods, playing sports, spending time with our children. Any activity that refreshes and uplifts our spiritual energy is good.

I have found daily meditation to be an indispensable, innocence-feeding daily activity. Before I start I may find myself beset by any manner of negative feelings and thoughts—fear, resentment, self-pity, selfish desires, and the like. But meditation stills the mind, and in the stillness, God is able to contact me and refresh me. He allows me to feel his love. I find this very nourishing and revitalizing.

Jesus also commands Jairus and the others to tell no one about the healing. Our relationship with the Lord's innocence is an internal and intimate one. To talk about the innocence that God gives us harms that very innocence. Pride, the antithesis of love's innocence, lurks within any discussion of how we are innocent or good. Besides, the opinions of others are irrelevant to the presence of the Lord's innocence within us. If we are seeking approval or acceptance, we are still suffering from the delusions of pride.

When we doubt our own innocence, very often we try to find reassurance and affirmation from other people. We try to fill our hearts with their love or with their approval. But no human being can fill up the emptiness inside. And unfortunately, such efforts often leave us feeling all the more wounded and spiritually dead.

Jesus is telling us that we don't need to go outside to find our innocence. We don't need anyone's approval. We don't need anybody's validation. The fact is that no matter how far down into hell we've gone, no matter how sick or dead our innocence may seem, our innocence lies within the inner chamber of the heart of our Lord Jesus, and it can be resurrected. In fact, from his perspective, it never even died. Rather than trying to gain a sense of innocence from the acceptance of others, we should do the exact opposite.

In the previous story, we learned that by being honest about our weaknesses we can overcome our fear of public shame. Here in this story we learn that by remaining silent we can overcome our need for the approval of the crowd. We don't brag about our spiritual progress.

The wonderful message Jesus offers us in this account is that he can and will restore innocence to our lives. He will resurrect our ability to feel clean and comfortable with ourselves. He will raise up our lost ability to look out into the world with simple wonder and gratitude. We can learn to love others selflessly without strings of neediness attached.

I once went skydiving from a small plane when a sophomore in college. We were trained on how to leave the aircraft's door and hold onto the wing strut. Once under the wing, we were to wait for the instructor's thumbs-up signal, at which point we were supposed to let go, arch back, and wait five seconds for the static line attached to the plane to open up our chutes. I remember the sinking feeling I had as I slowly inched out the door and clung for dear life to the wing strut. With a big grin, the instructor gave me the thumbs-up, but my hands didn't seem to want to let go. The teacher repeated the thumbs-up sign over and over, but my hands weren't moving. It was only when I thought he was about to come and pry me off the strut that I finally let go. Instantly blinded by sheer terror, I became convinced that my chute was broken and wasn't going to open. However, after about three seconds (each of which felt eternal), the chute opened and I floated serenely over the beautiful Iowa landscape, breathing in the crisp, clean air.

When we finally release our vice-like grip on the effort to save ourselves, we fall into a terror about our spiritual condition. However, following our spiritual flight instructor's command to "just let go and let God" liberates us into an awareness of a greater peace and expansive view of reality than we would have otherwise known.

These two healing accounts, the woman healed of a flow of blood and the raising of Jairus's daughter, are united to each other. Their applications in our lives today are likewise united. In the former, we learn to despair of our own efforts to become morally perfect. In the latter, we are awakened to the fact that innocence is not something we obtain through moral perfection; rather, innocence is a willingness to trust in the Lord, regardless of how bad things seem. This kind of innocence is imbued into us through experience.

It is quite possible that when we lead with our weakness and allow ourselves to be vulnerable with others, as the previous story urges, we will be judged. There is no guarantee that we will be well received despite our faults. Nevertheless, even this judgment can be considered a blessing. It forces the issue of what to believe. Do we invest our faith into the opinions and judgments of others, or do we rest our trust on the Lord of Love, whose yoke is easy and burden light? He always accepts us and is always eager to give us true, spiritual rest.

I have mentioned several times that these last three miracles are all related both as to their arrangement in the Bible and as to their spiritual message of healing. The overall lesson could be summed up as follows: Our addictions and bad habits are external forces that are more powerful than ourselves. We must give up on trying to overcome them by our own strength. We must be honest with others about our weaknesses, and we must trust in the Lord in each given moment, regardless of how bad it seems. In doing this, we will find that we are returned to sanity and empowered to live rightly.

MEDITATION

After entering into a meditative state, live through this story from the perspective of Jairus as fully as possible. Allow yourself to delve into the powerful emotions Jairus must have felt. How do you feel when the servants tell you that your daughter has died, that there is no need to trouble the teacher? In the face of a hopeless situation, allow yourself to feel childlike hope and trust in Jesus as you follow him. Listen to the scorn of the mourners. How do they make you feel? Watch as Jesus kicks them out. Again, what emotion do you feel? Now you enter into the inner room where you see your daughter lying apparently dead. What do you feel as you see her? Watch as Jesus takes her hand, and listen as he says, "Talitha cum!" Feel the elation as you see her arise. Embrace her and feed her.

LEAVES

1. Innocence is not purity and perfection.
2. Innocence is a willingness to trust in the Lord, no matter what.

3. Jesus can and will restore innocence to our lives if we are willing to trust.

4. Before this can happen, we must despair of the idea that we have any innate innocence or goodness of our own.

5. Self-pity and scorn are based in pride and hinder our trust in Jesus.

6. Our innocence is between ourselves and the Lord. We should not seek approval from others. We should not brag to others.

FRUIT

1. Whenever feelings of hopelessness, self-pity, scorn, worry, or fear arise, we notice them and place our trust into Jesus through a silent mental prayer: *Lord, I am powerless over this situation and these feelings. But I choose to trust in you no matter what.*

2. Practice letting go. At least once a day, empty your mind of all other worries and concerns and simply spend time trusting Jesus.

3. What does innocence mean to you? Spend some time reflecting on this as you go through your week. Write something about it if you feel moved to do so. Can you think of people in your life who embody this quality? What are they like?

DISCUSSION QUESTIONS

1. Did the Lord touch your life in any special way this week?

2. Did placing trust in the Lord in the face of trials have a noticeable effect?

3. Did you sense an increase of peace?

4. Did the meditation prove useful?

5. What trials have you faced that made you question your faith?

6. Can you remember a time when you felt your innocence had died? Are you having trouble asking the Lord to restore it? If so, why?

6

HEALING FROM DOUBT

"I believe; help my unbelief!"

Mark 9:14–29

When they came to the disciples, they saw a great crowd around them, and some scribes arguing with them. When the whole crowd saw him, they were immediately overcome with awe, and they ran forward to greet him. He asked them, "What are you arguing about with them?"

Someone from the crowd answered him, "Teacher, I brought you my son; he has a spirit that makes him unable to speak; and whenever it seizes him, it dashes him down; and he foams and grinds his teeth and becomes rigid; and I asked your disciples to cast it out, but they could not do so."

He answered them, "You faithless generation, how much longer must I be among you? How much longer must I put up with you? Bring him to me."

And they brought the boy to him. When the spirit saw him, immediately it convulsed the boy, and he fell on the ground and rolled about, foaming at the mouth. Jesus asked the father, "How long has this been happening to him?"

And he said, "From childhood. It has often cast him into the fire and into the water, to destroy him; but if you are able to do anything, have pity on us and help us."

Jesus said to him, "If you are able!—All things can be done for the one who believes." Immediately the father of the child cried out, "I believe; help my unbelief!"

When Jesus saw that a crowd came running together, he rebuked the unclean spirit, saying to it, "You spirit that keeps this boy from speaking and hearing, I command you, come out of him, and never enter him again!"

After crying and convulsing him terribly, it came out, and the boy was like a corpse, so that most of them said, "He is dead." But Jesus took him by the hand and lifted him up, and he was able to stand.

When he had entered the house, the disciples asked him privately, "Why could we not cast it out?" He said to them, "This kind can come out only through prayer."

<hr>

"I believe; help my unbelief!" With eyes full of tears and a heart full of love, the desperate father cried out this paradoxical plea. The emotion of the moment and the power of the man's passion for his son remain moving even today, thousands of years later. And the healing power of Jesus's words is also equally real and powerful today.

Many of us can very much relate to the fervent cry of the father: "I believe, help my disbelief!" We want to have faith, but we also have doubts. Doubts come in a multitude of shapes and sizes, but they all pose significant barriers to our spiritual progress. They interfere with our peace; they disturb our ability to feel the Lord's presence and love in our lives. They inhibit our ability to touch the lives of others in positive ways. And they are not easy to simply dismiss. In fact, we can no more dismiss these doubts through our own strength than the disciples could cast the epileptic demon from the boy in this story.

The preceding five chapters of this book have made astonishing promises. Each chapter, in fact, has proclaimed possible a kind of personal change that can best be labeled and understood with the word "miracle." By definition, a miracle defies reason. A miracle is a positive event that can in no way be achieved by human or natural strength alone. Miracles transcend and confound both our power and our intellect. Miracles, therefore, inherently give rise to doubt.

So far, this book has offered the following:

1. Freedom from a sense of unworthiness
2. Freedom from an unforgiving spirit
3. Freedom from addictions and bad habits
4. Freedom from inner warfare
5. A resurrected innocence

Before these healings occur, it is a given that as sufferers, we will doubt that Jesus can cure us. We have exhausted our every resource and expended our last ounce of energy in an effort to change, but find that we are no better off than when we began. If anything, our constant and sure failure has drained us entirely of hope, annihilated our morale, and left us utterly defeated.

Those readers who do not suffer such ailments may not be able to understand why these restorations would seem so impossible; *after all*, they may think, *if I am at peace, why can't anybody be so?* A student quick to understand algebra may not understand why his peer continually fails to understand basic concepts regardless of his effort. But those readers who are aware of their spiritual infirmities will understand the deep despair of which I speak.

Most of us do experience doubt of some kind. We may wonder if the Lord is real, or if he can really improve our lives. Yet we do want to believe. Like the father of the epileptic boy in this story, we want to believe that the miracles can occur. Of course we want to live! This hope and desire is enough if we are willing to follow it through and beyond our stubborn disbelief.

Jesus is sending his healing and love out to us all the time, but to the extent that our eyes, hands, and hearts are closed by doubt, we are unable to accept his grace. Our lack of faith that Jesus can heal us inhibits us from receiving his miraculous and curative love. And on our own, we can't overcome doubts. Thus it is a great miracle when

Jesus heals us of faltering faith, and in so doing opens us up to the wondrous salve and joy of his love. This story can be understood as his hands reaching out to heal us of doubt.

The story opens with an unknown heated argument between the scribes and the disciples. Who were the scribes? The scribes were very learned individuals—the intellectual elite of the day. They were necessarily highly intelligent in order for them to have advanced through the upper echelons of education. Their education secured them high positions in Jewish government. Scribes generally served as judges, lawyers, and teachers. Thus they had no lack of reason to feel intelligent and powerful. These feelings were amplified many times by the fact that Jewish government and civil law were the same as Jewish religious law. The scribes spent their entire lives studying the Old Testament, the law of God. They were not only the masters of government and learning, they were masters of God's truth. What they knew, they believed to be God's divine dictates. When they expounded upon the law, they believed they were the spokesmen of Yahweh himself. It's easy to understand why they had such difficulty accepting Jesus's teaching and his authority. He didn't fit their expectations for the Messiah. His preaching didn't fall in line with their vision of reality. They had difficulty imagining that their version of the truth might be incorrect. After all, they were the experts!

Many of us find that our heads are full of such scribes. Western and global cultures are increasingly based upon scientific materialism. Ours is a highly educated society. Throughout our school days we are taught to define reality according to what can be tested, repeated, and proved with the senses. Our minds have been trained and chained into this very limited, materialistic paradigm. This impoverished vision of reality is very powerful because it makes non-materialistic visions of reality seem to be groundless and delusional. Having been raised to understand reality from within this scientific, materialism paradigm, though I went to church and loved the topic of religion, I found my head constantly filled with doubts and arguments against God. These scribes of our minds refuse to accept the validity of God without undeniable proof. They insist on seeing before they believe.

God wants us to understand and know him intellectually. There is nothing wrong with searching to know God. He even encourages it: "Search, and you will find" (Matt. 7:7 and Luke 11:9); "Come unto me . . . and learn of me" (Matt. 11:28, 29); "Come let us reason together" (Isa. 1:18). God gives us intelligence and he wants us to use it. The problem arises when, rather than serving as an avenue to God, we make our own intelligence out to be God. We refuse to believe anything we can't prove. We define reality by what we can understand. This attitude gives rise to the scribes within us.

Reality is much bigger than what we can understand, of course. The world of science has repeatedly had to draw and redraw the paradigm by which we understand the natural universe. And surely there will be no end to the flaws and limits of our understanding. Just when we think we've got it figured out, some other discovery will blow the old idea out of the water. But all science-alone paradigms, I'm convinced, blind our minds to other, fuller ways of interacting with God's creation. The scientific mindset asks, "How does it work?" It focuses our mind on seeing things in a linear, temporal, and very materialistic way. I am also convinced that the science-alone paradigm arises from a lust for power. We want to be able to manipulate and control reality according to our will. This underlying goal causes us to see and interact with reality according to a master-slave relationship in which we are masters and reality is the slave. We see reality in terms of how we can control it. Our lust for power causes us to think of reality as mechanical and therefore manipulable. If we were to see reality as a living, sacred being—which is what I believe reality to be—we would no longer feel comfortable treating her as a machine. We would become aghast at the abuse we've leveled against her.

In opposition to the science-alone paradigm, which asks, "How does it work?" and "How can I control it?" consider this question: "How can I best serve and love you?" If we focus on this question, life suddenly appears much different from the machinery of quarks, chemicals, and electromagnetism that science describes. Now we see that reality is God's love dancing. We are filled with awe, enchantment, and holy wonder. We love where once we manipulated. It's not that our understanding of reality has expanded, it's that we are feeling and interacting with life with more of our being than mere intellect. We can let go of paradigms and decided to engage with reality authentically in each moment. Science and reason are still there with us, but they are no longer the sole lens through which we see.

None of this is to say science is bad; rather, it is to say that science must be subservient to love. Our intellect is not up to the task of deciding the nature of reality. The more we study, the less we know—the mysteries of the universe keep expanding. Using the intellect to define reality is like building four windowless walls around us and believing that reality is only what we can see within the box. We must instead use our heart.

Just as the scribes trusted more in their interpretation of the Law of Moses than the power of God, so some of us have the tendency to trust not so much in God, but in our own ability to understand God. Thoughts about God should complement and add depth to faith; but faith should not rely on intellectual proof of God. The first commandment forbids us to make, worship or serve any idol "whether in the form of anything that is in heaven above, or that is on the earth beneath, or that is in the water under the earth" (Exod. 20:4) or to worship any God other than Yahweh. We can think of our thoughts as idols of reality: they aren't reality itself, but replicas. So it is also with our thoughts about God. God tells us in the first commandment not to give these thought images too much importance, but to worship Yahweh alone.

One of the ways God leaves us in freedom is to remain impervious to proof one way or another. We can no more prove God with science and senses then we can disprove him. And what other option does God really have? He can't allow himself to be proved, otherwise, we'd lose our freedom—our freedom to not believe. Nor can he allow himself to be disproved. This is the way it must be. Those who search and want to believe find ample reason to believe. Those who wish to disbelieve and turn away from God are able to do so.

Many of us who do have doubts arising in our minds are not without moments of strong faith. On the contrary, we may have had powerful experiences in which we felt the undeniable power of Jesus within our lives. Perhaps a loved one was miraculously cured after a lot of prayer. Perhaps we felt the strong leading of the Holy Spirit. At those times, we might have thought, *I could never possibly doubt again!* and yet, a few days later we find ourselves questioning Jesus—*again!* We have seen that the more we trust and believe in Jesus, the better our lives become, and still the doubts give us no rest. But for those of us who suffer the tyranny of these interminable scribes, there is a solution. This story has the power to heal us of our doubts.

I have personally experienced the healing power of this story. Despite countless strong experiences of God's gracious guidance and mercy in my life—some were even miraculous—I still found my thoughts getting entangled in debates over the validity of Jesus as God and over the value of worshiping Jesus. A few years after having meditated deeply on the healing message of this miracle for the first time, I can honestly say that I now very rarely doubt the Lord of Love.

In the story, the scribes are arguing with the disciples. Similarly, in our minds, intellectual self-reliance argues with faith. Until we discover the healing power that Jesus has for us within this story, these scribes give us no peace. It's not that we want to doubt. In fact, many of us want to believe more fully. But the doubts enter without invitation and disturb our desired faith. Many things cause us doubt. We see injustice and suffering, and we begin to waver. Our fervent and earnest prayers for the healing of a loved one go unanswered. We've tried our best to follow Jesus, but things don't seem any better.

The scribes within our mind also attack our faith by blaming our problems on our faith:

- Maybe I am deluded . . . Maybe my faith is keeping me in the intellectual dark . . . Maybe I could be more clever or successful if I didn't believe.
- Perhaps if I didn't think so much about God, I'd have more peace and could just do what I wanted to do, enjoy life simply.
- If there is a God, he obviously doesn't love me.
- How could the God of the universe walk on our little earth? How could he rise bodily? If Jesus is God, why hasn't he returned as he promised?

Out of the midst of the argument between the scribes and the disciples, a man comes to Jesus and pleads that he heal his son. The boy is possessed by evil spirits. The symptoms of this possession are very similar to the symptoms of epileptic seizures. In fact, some translations of the Bible specify that the boy's ailment is epilepsy. When Jesus asks the man if he believes, the man cries out, "I believe; help my unbelief!" Here God is communicating with us through the words of the man; God is telling us that he understands our problem—we believe, but we also don't believe. We have a lot of doubts. Jesus then commands the "deaf and dumb" spirit to leave the body of the poor boy.

The argument between the scribes and the disciples mirrors the dilemma of the father—a war between faith and doubt. The disciples believe, but the scribes doubt. The man's mind is likewise divided between faith and doubt. The possession of the boy itself is symbolic of the same problem. Modern science has proved that the worst cases of "drop epilepsy" (epilepsy characterized by seizures that cause the subject to fall and seize, as was the case of this boy) can be treated by disallowing communication between the two hemispheres in the brain. This shows that in severe drop epilepsy, the two sides of the brain are not functioning properly as one organ. There is some kind of miscommunication between the two sides. One theory is that each side receives and then amplifies communication from the other before sending it back. Thus an inappropriate escalation of electrochemical signals occurs. The left hemisphere is responsible for logic and reasoning. The right has a more affection- and image-based vision of reality. Thus in this kind of epilepsy, we see a physical representation of the spiritual battle between "logical" doubt and intuitive faith. These two opposite ways of viewing life miscommunicate with one another, leading to an escalation of tension until we are spiritually incapacitated.

Thus, this story contains a multilayered fractal: within the boy, the two sides of the brain are warring against each other (or the demons are warring against the boy's "right" mind); the man's doubts are warring against his faith; the scribes are warring against the disciples; and in our lives, our intellectual pride may be warring against our faith that Jesus can heal us by means of this miracle.

If we find that doubting thoughts are constantly cropping up in our minds, we too are suffering a form of spiritual epilepsy that only Jesus can heal. This very story opens the door to Jesus and his healing. Jesus can and will exorcise this spirit out of us in the same way he did for this boy. If we suffer from inner warfare between faith and doubt, the first thing we need to do is acknowledge that we are suffering from what amounts to spiritual epilepsy. On our own, we have no more power to overcome and heal ourselves from this spiritual disease than did the disciples to cast out the demon from the boy. Having come to see and acknowledge our disease and need of help, we need to emulate the father of the boy and simply confess the truth about our mental state to the Lord in prayer: "I believe; help my unbelief." We admit to Jesus that while we have a lot of doubt, we also have enough faith to ask him to remove or override that doubt.

This need not be a one-time event. We can go through this short prayer at the beginning of every day if we sense that those inner scribes are still vying to control our consciousness. Sometimes we need to repeat the prayer during the course of the day if we encounter something or someone that stimulates doubt.

Personally, I have found that if I admit my lack of faith and ask Jesus to help, he invariably answers my prayer and gives rest to my heart. I instantly feel a strong and happy trust in Jesus. I used to try to intellectually dispel my doubts. Arguments pro and con for God would rage through my mind days, weeks, months, and even years on end. I thought the answer to doubt would arise in the form of an intellectual concept—an idea so grand that all doubts would be forever dispersed. It never happened. I could not think my way out of that state of doubt. Jesus, in this miracle, showed me, and shows anyone interested, that the way to overcome doubt is to pray to him for help.

In my personal experience, I found that I had to pray for help about wavering faith daily for about one month. But after a month or so, I saw that my faith was much steadier. After years of wavering, this simple prayer has allowed Jesus to give me serenity of faith. It is a miraculous healing in light of the fact that I had tried and failed for well over twenty years to strengthen my faith on my own.

I still need to pray for this healing on occasion, especially after having read literature that challenges my faith in some way. I also need to ask for this healing when I come across what seems an insurmountable life challenge, be it an external situation or an internal one. I need to pray for faith that with his help, I can overcome.

In the previous healing account, Jesus commanded the parents of the little girl, "Do not fear, only believe!" Sometimes it is difficult for us to believe that our innocence can be restored. We feel kinship with those who scoffed outside. It seems God knows that we may have trouble mustering up our faith. Following that healing, this account gently teaches us how to dispel our doubts and open our heart to full belief that Jesus can restore our innocence. He knows that our innocence is not dead, but sleeping, and that he can awaken it to life again.

It might help us to remember that Jesus not only healed the boy of the evil spirit, but at the same moment, he healed the father of his doubt. Jesus healed them both. His miracle likely silenced the doubting scribes as well. He can heal us in the same way. Rather than trying to fight doubt with our own reasoning, as we did in the past, we give our doubts over to Jesus. Rather than trying to bolster faith with thought, we surrender to Jesus in prayer. The ensuing dramatic and miraculous increase in our previously shaky faith only causes us to believe all the more. "Once God has spoken; twice I have heard this: power belongs to God" (Ps. 62:11).

We may have feared that too much faith would blind us from reality, from the truth. But truth isn't merely an intellectual thing. The real proof of any truth is its effectiveness in producing peace, love, and harmony, both within an individual and within society at large. Without a doubt, faith in the Lord produces more inner peace than anything else I've ever known—and I've searched high and low. And without a doubt, to the extent I rest my mind in the Lord, to that extent I am more attuned to how to respond to people around me in ways that are loving, peaceful, and healing.

The disciples asked Jesus why they couldn't cast the demon out from the boy. We, too, may have wondered why we were constantly plagued by doubts despite our effort to believe and be good disciples. That faithful part of us, represented by the disciples, just isn't powerful enough to neutralize the doubts within. We were trying to counter all the internal anti-faith arguments with arguments in favor of Jesus. But that isn't how this particular battle can be won. As Jesus told his disciples, "This kind can come out only through prayer." Rather than engaging in an intellectual debate with our doubts, we simply get on our knees and admit the truth, "Lord, I believe. I also have doubts. Please heal me of the doubts."

In some versions of this story, Jesus says that casting out the demon requires both prayer and fasting. Fasting is an undeniable sign that an individual is willing to believe in Jesus over and above the reality of this earth alone. The body, which is of the earth, wants to eat food. When we temporarily refuse this most basic drive, we show to both God and ourselves that we are willing to let God be the master of our lives, over and above the nonspiritual motivations exemplified by our desire to eat.

Because fasting is such an uncommon practice in modern society, its importance is not recognized. A day or more without food

can do wonders for realigning our minds and hearts onto the spiritual path of God, the Way of Yahweh. When we get stuck in some form
of selfishness or when we can't surrender a problem over to God, a
period of time without food in conjunction with prayer, meditation,
and scriptural reading powerfully loosens the bonds that trap our
spirit. The reward is an increased sense of closeness with God and
the dissipation of doubts that block our spiritual serenity.

I have fasted on occasion when facing more extreme problems,
and I never felt that it was a waste of time or a useless discomfort.
The discomfort has invariably turned out to be a small price paid for
the spiritual benefit I've gained. I have always come out the other
side with a heightened awareness of God's presence, love, and guidance in my life.

But most of the time, prayer is enough to overcome doubts. In
retrospect, it seems so simple and obvious—*admit doubts and pray
for help!* But after years of captivity within the walls of doubt, to be
free from fearful second-guessing—spiritual epilepsy—is nothing
short of miraculous for me. I tried my best to know and believe in
God. But all along, all that was required was that I admit to the Lord
the truth, and pray for him to help me with my disbelief.

MEDITATIONS

1. After entering into a meditative state of mind, put yourself in
the shoes of the father in this story. Your son has been ill for many
years, and his destructive fits are getting worse and worse. You fear
he will die. Hearing of the wonderful healing powers of Jesus, you
seek him out. But he is not there, only his disciples. You watch as
they try to cast out the demon, but they cannot. As your hopes with-
er, you hear the disciples begin to argue with some nearby scribes.
Suddenly, the crowd parts, and a man says, "What are you arguing
about with them?" This must be Jesus! Immediately you come forward and explain the problem. "All things can be done for the one
who believes," he tells you.

Doubt seizes you. Do you believe? Is your faith strong enough after so many disappointments? But you see your son, and know you must believe, for his sake. "I believe!" you cry out to Jesus. "Help my unbelief!" Jesus smiles, understanding your struggle and your faith, and commands the demon to come out of your son. Your son convulses horribly, and in your mind, the voice of doubt whispers, "He will die." You push the thought away and focus on belief. The convulsions stop. Jesus reaches out his hand, and your son stands. He is healed. All doubts are banished.

2. After entering into a meditative state of mind, imagine yourself as a son or daughter resting in your father's arms after having been healed of epilepsy. As you do this, know that your father is the Lord of Love.

3. After arriving at a meditative state of mind, meditate on reality as a living being to be honored as the ever-unfolding expression of Divine Love.

LEAVES

1. Life is not a machine.
2. Life is a living expression of God's love.
3. Doubts are best handled by prayer, not rational argument.

FRUIT

1. When confronted by doubts, we get on our knees, confess our doubts and pray for their removal.

2. If we have constitutional doubts, we start each day with prayers for healing of our doubts.

3. If it is difficult to have emotional faith in any of the following issues, we can pray for help on these:

• God is real.
• Jesus is God.

- He knows us all.
- He loves us all.
- He wills and is able to heal us of our emotional and spiritual problems.
- The Word is Christ manifested with us.

4. If we are confronted by an issue that causes undue doubt or a problem that we have trouble inviting God into, we can fast for twenty-four hours, taking time to bring the issue to God.

5. We practice interacting with reality as a sacred and living image of Divine Love rather than as a machine.

DISCUSSION QUESTIONS

1. Has anything remarkable happened to you this week; did the Lord touch you this week in a special way concerning or not concerning the message of this miracle?

2. What was your experience of the meditations?

3. What was your experience of the exercises?

4. Has there ever been a time when your faith in God was challenged? How did you overcome it?

5. Do you find the arguments of science compelling? Do you see science and religion as fundamentally compatible or incompatible?

6. If any value was gained from this miracle, how can we incorporate it and sustain it in our daily lives?

7

HEALING FROM FAITH-ARROGANCE

"But only speak the word, and let my servant be healed."

Luke 7:1–10

After Jesus had finished all his sayings in the hearing of the people, he entered Capernaum. A centurion there had a slave whom he valued highly, and who was ill and close to death. When he heard about Jesus, he sent some Jewish elders to him, asking him to come and heal his slave.

When they came to Jesus, they appealed to him earnestly, saying, "He is worthy of having you do this for him, for he loves our people, and it is he who built our synagogue for us."

And Jesus went with them, but when he was not far from the house, the centurion sent friends to say to him, "Lord, do not trouble yourself, for I am not worthy to have you come under my roof; therefore I did not presume to come to you. But only speak the word, and let my servant be healed. For I also am a man set under authority, with soldiers under me, and I say to one, 'Go,' and he goes, and to another, 'Come,' and he comes, and to my slave, 'Do this,' and the slave does it."

When Jesus heard this he was amazed at him, and turning to the crowd that followed him, he said, "I tell you, not even in Israel have I found such faith." When those who had been sent returned to the house, they found the slave in good health.

~~~

In the last chapter we learned how to let Jesus heal us of wavering faith. Once we decide to surrender our doubts to God, the next hurdle we run into in our spiritual journey is a misunderstanding of what faith is all about. This chapter shows how to move beyond the roadblock of self-based faith.

Let's start by taking a look at this centurion. Here's a man with a big heart. We can see this in the fact that he built a synagogue for the Jews. In the giving of this very large gift, a lot of information about the centurion is revealed. First, it shows us that the centurion had a deep interest in and appreciation for Jewish religion. He could have built a sports arena, a park, or a music hall. Instead, he built a house of worship, showing that he had an active interest and reverence for Judaism and, more importantly, a love for Yahweh. Second, his gift shows us that he was extremely generous. Deep appreciation for the Jewish religion certainly doesn't demand that a gift be offered, let alone so costly a gift as a synagogue.

It's easy to appreciate something without contributing of ourselves to it. We may appreciate health, but don't exercise or eat right. We may like a clean house, but can't be bothered with the cleaning. We might like the ideal of spiritual development and fortitude, but we find ourselves distracted and occupied by more "urgent" or "practical" tasks. And this leads us to the third conclusion about this centurion: he was a man of action. He was not content to simply feel appreciation. He wanted to show his appreciation with action. He made his affection real in the material world.

Fourth and finally, we see that this centurion was a very humble individual. Occupying the tiny, backwater state of Israel, it would have been quite expected for a military official of the Roman Empire, the mightiest organization on earth at the time, to feel superior to his subjects and treat them with prideful disdain. Not so this man.

In his dealings with the Jews, he showed utmost respect and regard. He not only built them a synagogue, but it is obvious from the text that he had a good relationship with them. Good relationships only arise in an atmosphere of respect and appreciation.

As we have already observed, like the centurion, Jewish leaders also held positions of power and prestige. But, looking at almost all the interactions between Jesus and these Jewish leaders, we know that unlike this centurion, the power and prestige they enjoyed went to their heads. They burdened the common people with loads too heavy to bear. They loved the best seats in the synagogues. Sounding their trumpets to announce their deeds, they reveled in the reverence and respect that the common people offered them. They even took offerings that by law were intended for the parents of those who offered them. While Jewish leaders used their position to gain privilege, power, prestige, and possessions for themselves, the centurion used his position to give respect, honor, and a new synagogue to others.

Before we get puffed up and look down on the Jewish elders, we would be wise to recall that these same tendencies and traits exist in our own minds as well. In fact, if we feel superior to the Jewish leaders, that very feeling of superiority betrays the fact that we suffer the same spiritual ailment they did—arrogance.

The centurion was not arrogant. The humility of this centurion is illustrated even more clearly in the fact that he did not feel worthy even to have Jesus come to his house. We do not know what this man's house was like, but we can be certain that it was no hovel. Having enough money to build a synagogue, he surely had enough for a fine home. He probably lived in relative luxury. It was not a problem with his home that made him feel unworthy to host Jesus. Rather, it was that he knew Jesus to be holy.

The centurion's humility was not based in insecurity or self-loathing. We know from his own words that the centurion was accustomed to commanding people and he demanded obedience—not the attitude or activity of a person plagued by self-abasing recrimination. He didn't humble himself before Jesus because he deprecated himself, but because he knew who Jesus was and revered him in the way the Lord of Love deserves to be revered.

The centurion knew Jesus was God incarnate. He had a more profound insight into this truth than any other. Jesus's words confirm this: "I tell you, not even in Israel have I found such faith." Having deep respect for Jewish religion, it is likely this centurion knew the Jewish prophecies of a coming savior. From the amount of faith this man invested in Jesus, we can assume that he believed Jesus to be that savior, Emmanuel: God with us.

Feeling unworthy to be in the presence of Jesus, the centurion sends the "Jewish elders" as liaisons for him. Now this is where the story becomes fascinating. The elders plead with Jesus on behalf of this Roman. Something isn't adding up. Think of it: *Jewish leaders pleading with Jesus? On behalf of a Roman ruler?*

There is nowhere else in the New Testament where Jewish leaders humble themselves enough to ask Jesus for help. Nicodemus interacted with the Lord in a somewhat positive way, but only under the cover of night. Nor is there anywhere else in the New Testament where Jewish leaders are interested in helping a Roman. In nearly every other account, the Jewish leaders despise both Rome and Jesus.

In a sense, the miracle has already taken place. That Jewish leaders would supplicate Jesus on behalf of a Roman official is at least a minor miracle. And here we get to the heart of the message and gain the insight we need to understand the personal application of this healing miracle. As our faith grows, we enter into a closer and more intimate conscious relationship with God, our Savior. As we grow closer to God in tangible ways, we too, like the centurion and like the Jewish leaders, enter into a position of privilege. It is indeed a privilege to believe in God deeply. It is a privilege to feel his presence with us. It is a privilege to say with confidence, "I know God loves me."

The question we now face is, *how do we deal with this position of privilege and power?* Do we fold this growing experience of God into our ego, and become arrogant, or do we, like the centurion, try to give it away and help others?

One of the first pitfalls we encounter as we begin to grow along spiritual lines is that we take pride in the positive steps God has produced within our lives. We feel important in our new relationship with God. We tend to grasp onto these advances as if they were our own achievements. We start feeling as if we are special or "chosen." But if we get caught up in this attitude, we will lose our place of privilege. We'll lose our connection with God. Trying to own God's grace is like catching a butterfly in our hands. Just as the oils and pressure of the hand damage the wings of the creature so that it can no longer fly, attaching our sense of self to God's grace in our lives ruins the grace so that it can no longer fly within our souls.

Instead, we have to follow the example of the Roman centurion. He obviously believed that Jesus was the Messiah. But he also knew himself to be an outsider. He knew that he was very fortunate and blessed to have come to know Yahweh and his earthly manifestation, Jesus. He expressed his gratitude in action and generosity. He took his faith and put it to work.

In contrast, we know from the New Testament that many Jewish leaders thought their position alone was enough for their salvation. This is a major hurdle we must similarly overcome. Let's not think that being in the "club" is enough. There is a strong vein of thought within Christianity that says just believing that Christ died for our sins is enough to be saved. Or we may unconsciously feel that we are saved because we have the right religious or spiritual knowledge. Or we may feel that we are saved because we do a lot of good things for others. We may feel we are saved because we refrain from sin. In one sense, each of these beliefs, usually subconscious, is a fractured aspect of truth.

Some religious folks debate whether it is faith or works that saves. Still others say that true faith is defined by the works it produces, thus faith is only as real as the works it produces. Jesus echoes this sentiment when he says that a tree is known by its fruit.

However, my understanding is that none of these explanations are fully true. Both from scriptures and from my life experience, I have come to fully believe that neither faith nor works, nor a combination of these things, save; rather, it is Jesus, the Lord of Love, who saves. He says, "You did not choose me but I chose you. And I appointed you to go and bear fruit, fruit that will last, so that the Father will give you whatever you ask him in my name" (John 15:16). In other words, Jesus calls us to faith, and that faith animates us from within to perform good works of love.

Whether we believe that salvation comes from faith, works, or some combination of the two, we will end up taking credit for our salvation. We will say either *my faithfulness saves me* or *my morality and good deeds save me*. In both cases, we have made ourselves into spiritual thieves. We are stealing from God what is only God's: the salvation of our soul. If we have faith, it is because God arranged for us to have faith. He instilled faith into our hearts. If we are moral and do good deeds from a motivation of genuine love, then it is because God, who is Love, has inspired us with love. The heart of the problem is in believing ourselves to be the prime source of our motivation toward faith and good deeds. Both faith and genuinely good actions arise from genuine love alone. And genuine love has only one source: the Lord.

What is salvation, anyway? Salvation is a state of mind that produces a way of being. Having a heart full of love is salvation. Love alone produces true joy and lasting peace. True love inspires us to refrain from harming others and to be fruitful. God is Love and Love is God. To the extent love has come to reside within our hearts, God has visited us with his salvation. Thus salvation is a never-ending, progressive process. Our capacity to grow in love is never exhausted.

Where does faith come into play? Faith, as explored in the introduction to this book, is faith in the value of Love as the essence of Jesus, and so of God. Love is what is truly human. Love is the source and creator of our humanity and all of reality. Faith is a willingness to subordinate all other motives and values under the authority and direction of Love as Divine. Love is not a nebulous quality. Love is intelligent, communicative, human, and Divine. We can know this because Love is what makes us intelligent and human and communicative. Thus it authors our humanity and so is Divine. Divine Love communicated himself to us as Jesus, and Jesus is the model and prototype of what it means to be loving. Thus faith in Jesus means that we attempt to give Jesus authority over our lives. And Jesus's command is that we love one another as he has loved us, which is to say that we lay down our selfish ends for the sake of serving the well-being of all. Love is the well-being of all.

And to the extent we give the Lord of Love authority in our lives, we will come to experience in a personal way the words of Jesus quoted above: we don't choose Jesus, he chooses us. In other words, we don't have faith in Love from motives arising from our personhood. Rather, Love moved us to faith through a combination of the loving experiences of our lives and the true ideas about Love that we were given to learn. Jesus causes us to have faith. Then, from that faith, he causes us to bear fruit, just as he promises to do in the Gospel. We will feel this as true when it begins to happen to us. And it happens to us this way according to God's timetable.

Thus we have absolutely nothing about which to feel arrogant in relation to our spiritual lives. On the contrary, the spirituality of love forces us to admit we can claim nothing good as our own doing.

We may mistakenly believe this means that we have to wait for God's influx or inspiration to flow into our lives—that God alone achieves salvation and we are just empty puppets. To believe this is to misunderstand the fundamental nature of Love. Divine Love is life itself, freedom itself, goodness itself, and activity itself. Thus when the Lord of Love imparts this life, freedom, and activity into us, we are then able to act in freedom to do good. And in this we are for the first time truly spiritually alive. In other words, when we believe in the Lord as Divine Love and when we choose to act according to what is loving, it will necessarily feel as if we are acting autonomously because freedom is the nature of Divine Love. We will sometimes even feel as if we are forcing ourselves to love despite a desire to be selfish. However, that sensation of choosing is a part of grace. Ultimately, the Lord alone animates us to faith and to good choices. The Lord of Love gives his life to us in such a way that it feels like it is ours. In giving his activity to us, we must act as if from our own being. We must work, but cannot lay claim to the motivation behind the work.

Without faith in the Lord as Love and Love as Lord, we can do nothing. Faith is an action. And faith is given to us as a free gift by the Lord of Love. If we take credit for "our" actions, faith, or good choices (such as choosing to believe) we pollute them with our self-glorifying ego just as the Pharisees and Jewish rulers polluted their privileged religious position. The Lord loves us; he forgives us; he knows exactly who we are and what we need. He is the way, the truth, and the life. His way is the way of love and is the only path to true peace and happiness.

Rather than faith serving us, we are to serve faith. The Lord revealed this idea very clearly when his disciples asked him about how to increase their faith (Luke 17:5). His response was to tell them a story about how a servant who, after working all day in the field, must come in and serve the master dinner before he himself may eat. Even after all of this, he should not expect a word of thanks, for he has done only what is required of him! This is a humbling answer, to say the least. Jesus is telling us is that to build faith, we must work hard and we must work not for the sake of reward, but because it is our duty.

Faith doesn't save us from the hard work of applying our lives to the discipline Jesus teaches us. On the contrary, faith is what inspires us to get going and try. If we don't have faith, we have no motivation to carry out Jesus's commands and instructions for us. Faith gives us the reason to work. The measure of faith is seen in the measure of work. Jesus said this in several ways: "They who have my commandments and keep them are those who love me" (John 14:21). "Those who love me will keep my word . . . Whoever does not love me does not keep my words" (John 14:23–24). "You are my friends if you do what I command you . . . I am giving you these commands so that you may love one another" (John 15:14, 17). "If you continue in my word, you are truly my disciples" (John 8:31). The spiritual path cannot be tread without discipline and duty.

Confession of faith, no matter how earnest and sincere, does not alone lift us out of hell into heaven. We can believe in Jesus and still be stuck in the hell of sin. Sin itself is hell. It doesn't matter if we are Christian, atheist, Hindu, or a New Ager; if we are caught up in sin, that sin creates hell in our lives. If I say, "I'm saved in Christ," but my life is full of the misery inherent within sin, what difference do my empty words make?

Faith in Jesus as Christ is just the first step. It is faith in the Lord of Love that allows us to invest effort into learning his ways and begin the hard work of applying ourselves to that work. If we don't have faith, why would we want to deny ourselves and carry the cross daily? Why would we want to turn the other cheek? Why would we want to lay down our lives for the sake of others? Embarking upon the Christian spiritual journey is learning how to become selfless. It takes a lot of faith to be willing to put down our self-based concerns and interests for the sake of loving other people. Surrendering our resentments, insecurities, and cravings all require sacrifices—sacrifices that would be impossible to make without faith. There is nothing more challenging than the Christian journey. Not only is it the hardest path, it is the longest, because it is never completed. We can always grow in love.

The centurion was an outsider to the nation and he was a man of action. This reveals the transition we have to make to receive this healing from Jesus. First, we have to learn to think of ourselves as fortunate foreigners who may receive God's grace and healing, though we are undeserving. As soon as we begin believing we are special or deserving because of our relationship with God, our faith, or our deeds, we lose our way. In and of ourselves, we are completely lost in selfishness and therefore sin. Like the centurion, we truly are foreigners to God's kingdom. We do not deserve God's love. We don't earn it. We are given it despite ourselves, and so we are unimaginably blessed.

Second, we have to put our money where our mouth is. We have to make our faith real in action. Just as the centurion's humble faith motivated him to gift the Jewish people with a synagogue, so we must perform the actions of service that faith demands of us.

In this account, a servant is ill, near death. Faith is the servant. The illness is pride. The Jewish leaders were supposed to have been servants both to God and to the common Jewish people. However, many were so full of pride that they were unable to properly serve and fulfill their duties to God and his people. As servants, they were spiritually ill and near death. There is a parallel between the centurion's sick servant and the Jewish leaders, who were spiritually sick servants. When our faith is prideful, we too are sick and able to properly serve neither God nor our fellows.

This is the sole account in the entire New Testament where the Jewish leaders humbly approach Jesus and ask for help. We have to ask ourselves what caused the change in their attitude. Why were these men humble rather than prideful? Why were they willing to plead with Jesus for help on behalf of a Roman? The answer is written within the text—it is because the centurion "loves our people and . . . built our synagogue for us." The humble, generous actions of the centurion healed the Jewish leaders of their arrogance. And in turn, their actions—their pleading with Jesus—led to the healing of the Roman's servant.

The centurion didn't owe the Jewish nation anything. He didn't need to build them a synagogue, but he did. He valued actions of love more than he valued his position or pride. The Jewish leaders in turn became willing to serve the centurion. The centurion's humility, expressed in action, was communicated to the Jewish leaders and transformed them into humble servants as well. That's the magic of love in action. When from faith we work to change ourselves and to bless other people, we open up a channel of communication between God and those we affect so that God's love can then inspire them to be more loving.

The centurion and the Jewish leaders were political enemies. Jesus tells us to love our enemies. For our purposes here, I am choosing to define "enemy" as anyone against whom we harbor hostility. We might slip into an attitude of hostility toward the woman who cuts us off on the road, the insurance telephone operator, the house repairman who overcharges for a shoddy job, tax collectors, political leaders, institutions, or those who are different from us. In all cases, it is our responsibility to love, to work for their well-being.

Sometimes our enemies are our closest loved ones. We may become hostile when faced with criticism from a spouse or the laziness of our children. If we examine such hostility, we will invariably find spiritual arrogance. We are judging others, insisting that they should be more spiritually evolved than we perceive them as being. We think they should be perfect, like ourselves. All spiritual judgment entails arrogance because only God is fit to judge. When we judge or are resentful of others, we are the ones with a problem. We can love our enemies by humbly working for their well-being.

The true expression of both faith and humility is revealed in actions of service toward other human beings. The first step in serving other people is cleansing our own life of actions and thoughts that are harmful to them and to our ability to love them. The second step is to begin looking and praying for ways to help others in their spiritual healing and development. The heart of a life of love in Jesus is that we "love one another." Jesus says that his true disciples will be recognized by their love.

Just as the centurion's servant was close to death, so too, arrogance causes our spirit to become very ill. A servant, of course, serves. He or she carries out the orders given by the master. When we think of ourselves as spiritually superior to others, we'll find that we have our relationship with God inverted. We are mistaking God for the servant and ourselves for the master. The essential action required by faith is a sustained, persistent effort to turn away from our arrogance. This is part of what it means to lay down our life for others.

The Lord of Love is the master, and we are the servants. The master shows us what he would have us do in his commandments, the chief of which is that we love one another as he has loved us. That's the command. As servants, it is up to us to get the job done. This book is about helping us to be spiritually healthy enough to get that job done.

Practice must take precedence over knowledge and position. And just as is true in all activities, we can't become expert in a day. It takes sustained effort through a long period of time for us to become good at being disciples of the Lord of Love. And we are never done learning or practicing how to love selflessly. There is always room for improvement.

The ultimate manifestation of the Word of God is loving activity between us. When we put ourselves in the servant's position and serve one another, we will find that changes occur in our lives. We will grow healthier spiritually. We will find states of peace and happiness increasingly filling our hearts. The servant—who represents all of us—is healed. We now can act out God's plan and will, whereas before we just wanted it to happen on its own accord.

We are foreigners, undeserving recipient of God's mercy. We are not the special elite. To keep spiritually healthy, we must remain humble servants. Constantly trying to let go of selfishness and so put our spiritual house in order is very effective in keeping us humble. As we read in James, "Just as the body without the spirit is dead, so faith without works is also dead" (James 2:26).

MEDITATION

After entering into a meditative state of mind, imagine yourself in the role of the Jewish elders. You are with the Roman in his house and his servant falls seriously ill. You marvel at how deeply the Roman cares for his servant. You also marvel at his humility as he explains that he doesn't feel worthy to approach Jesus and so asks you to intercede for the sake of his servant. You initially feel hesitant—on the one hand, to serve a Roman, and on the other to ask Jesus for help. But because this man has been good to the nation, building a synagogue, you swallow your pride and petition Jesus for help.

What feelings arise as Jesus agrees to come to the centurion's house? You see the centurion's friends coming. They stop Jesus and tell him that he need not come to the house, for the centurion knows Jesus can command the healing from afar. You feel humbled when Jesus says, "Not even in Israel have I found such faith." You return to the house of the Roman and find that his servant is completely healed. Notice what feelings you have.

LEAVES

1. Faith without works is dead, and so we are not saved by faith alone.

2. Faith in the Lord of Love means working for the sake of love. Faith does not exist to serve us, but rather faith inspires us to serve.

3. We are not special because of our faith or our progress, but forever undeserving servants and recipients of grace.

4. Just as the centurion knew that Jesus could heal via servants, so we realize that God works through us as his servants.

FRUIT

1. Do something to bless another person each day this week.

2. In prayer each day, acknowledge that you are a servant and a foreigner in God's kingdom; ask the Lord what you can do to serve him and other people this day.

3. Clean something that needs cleaning at least once this week.

DISCUSSION QUESTIONS

1. What positive feelings did you feel in relation to the exercises? What negative feelings arose?

2. What insights did you have this week in relation to the lesson?

3. What did you gain from the meditation?

4. Was it difficult for you to put yourself in the position of the Jewish elders? What positive results occurred when you did so?

5. Can you think of a time you felt arrogant about your own faith?

6. Could you do what the centurion did, and spend a significant portion of your own money to support a different community? What did you think as you reflected on that action?

7. What did you clean, and what results did you get?

8

HEALING FROM LACK OF JOY

"One of them turned back, praising God with a loud voice."

Luke 17:11–19

On the way to Jerusalem Jesus was going through the region between Samaria and Galilee. As he entered a village, ten lepers approached him. Keeping their distance, they called out, saying, "Jesus, Master, have mercy on us."

When he saw them, he said to them, "Go and show yourselves to the priests." And as they went, they were made clean.

Then one of them, when he saw that he was healed, turned back, praising God with a loud voice. He prostrated himself at Jesus's feet and thanked him. And he was a Samaritan.

Then Jesus asked, "Were not ten made clean? But the other nine, where are they? Was none of them found to return and give praise to God except this foreigner?"

Then he said to him, "Get up and go on your way; your faith has made you well."

Caused by the bacteria *mycobacterium leprae,* leprosy (also known as Hansen's disease) attacks peripheral nerves, including those of the eye, the nasal mucous membranes, and the skin. When the eye becomes infected, blindness is a possible outcome. Infection of the lining of the nose results in a chronically stuffed nose. In the skin, the bacteria causes hard, raised nodules or lesions. Muscle atrophy and deformity occur in later stages, and the weakened body is more vulnerable to secondary infections.

The symptoms of leprosy are highly visible and, if untreated, progress over the course of many years. For an individual suffering leprosy, the ability to sense the world around him or her steadily diminishes. The senses of smell, touch, and vision all slowly erode. In ancient Israel, compounding this loss of contact with the physical realm, the afflicted also lost contact with the social realm due to expulsion from society.

Sufferers of leprosy had very little to rejoice about. Ostracized, they were doomed to a slow death of numb isolation. So it is not surprising that the Samaritan in this account returned after his healing to give worship and thanks to Jesus. We may wonder why the other nine didn't do the same.

A successful antibiotic treatment for leprosy was first developed in the early 1940s, and in developed countries, leprosy is not a part of our modern experience. But today, countless numbers of people suffer a kind of spiritual leprosy—progressive, emotional numbness. We feel emotionally isolated from others. We cannot sense the purpose of life. Nor can we perceive the reality of God in our lives. With our sense of emotional connection muted, joy and gratitude erode to nothing.

Depression rates in America have been on the rise since 1915, and the average age of onset is getting progressively lower. I believe emotional leprosy often arises in relation to a spiritual pathogen that is rampant in modern American culture, one that is spreading throughout the world. The pathogen consists of two false beliefs that are intimately bound together. The first is that personal happiness is the goal of life. The second is that personal happiness can be obtained through what I call the five P's: possessions, position, pleasures, prestige, and power. It is hard to not be infected by this potent pathogen. We are bombarded by media with visual and verbal messages that promulgate these diseased beliefs. Because we can never find happiness from the five P's, and yet remain deluded that we can, we become trapped in an addictive cycle. We are driven to obtain more and more. Business marketers and advertisers cash in on our spiritual ailment by simultaneously feeding and tapping our delusional drive for the five P's.

Individualistic societies are a relatively new phenomenon. Traditional cultures were (and in some places still are) sustained by a sense of "we," over and above the importance of "I." What is good for the tribe or community is good for the individual. The emotional lives of all members are understood to be inherently bound together in mutual interdependence. Such emotional bonds are formed through caring and compassion. When we care about one another, the happiness of others becomes our own happiness and, conversely, the sorrow of another is likewise our own. In a society based on concern for the well-being of all, happiness arises from togetherness regardless of the circumstances. Even in the face of hardship, if we are surrounded by a community of people who care about us, there is sweetness within the sorrow. We are sustained until the hardships pass. Thus the ups and downs intrinsic to life on earth are transcended by the spiritual joy of community and care.

In contrast, as members of an individualistic society we are taught to focus on the five P's as the means to happiness. We are neither available to support others when they fall on hard times, nor are we supported when we face life's challenges. The emotional impact of financial and similar problems is conflated both by the lack of support and also by the fact that society has raised the five P's to unwarranted importance in our minds. It is telling that in 1929, when investors in New York lost all of their material wealth in the stock market crash there was a rash of suicides; at the same time on the other side of the continent, Native American tribes held huge Potlatch celebrations in which they intentionally gave away all their material wealth. Knowing that togetherness takes precedent over individual material gain, these tribes found joy in giving it all away.

Yet not all who are infected with individualistic materialism are depressed. There seem to be those who bear the symptoms for the whole society. In other words, though the pathogen is systematic within the culture, only a few people show the resulting symptoms. Correspondingly, and perhaps not coincidentally, it is estimated that 95 percent of the population is genetically immune to leprosy. *Mycobacterium leprae* may be present, but only a few people bear the symptoms. Thus when we are depressed or unhappy, we need not pour the salt of self-blame on the wounds of societal delusion. We are victims of a social problem, but we can take individual action to be cured.

When ensnared within the delusion of individualistic materialism, feelings of unhappiness or boredom trigger a feeling that we need to get something more into our lives. We need a doughnut, some clothes, a vacation, a new car, a new extreme sport, a new job, a new drug, a new wife, or a new self. The problem is that the pleasure found in acquisition is short lived. The level and duration of joy diminishes with each new gain, and we get trapped in a vortex; we feel as if we need more and more and more. Many of us raise our kids according to this ideal. We want to show we love them, and so we buy things for them. It is not that gifts are bad; gifts are nice. But they are no substitute for quality time spent together.

Individualistic materialism causes spiritual leprosy. The real underlying issue is a failure to understand the innate unity of all human beings. Jesus speaks to this unity in the Gospel of John when he prays that all might believe, and in believing be made one in him as he is one with God (John 17:20–21). The introduction of this book talks about the idea that God is Love; the oneness spoken of in Jesus's final prayer can only be achieved by Love. When Divine Love fills us and animates us, we feel connected to both God and others. We rejoice in the joy of others and we mourn their sorrows. This connection with others is accomplished by a connection with the

Lord of Love. And this unity of Love is the source of true joy and contentment. When this unity of Love is not sensed, a sad emptiness sets in. Love alone is able to fill the emotional void, and it does so in part by opening our awareness to the inherent unity of humanity. Because we are created by the Lord of Love to be eternally happy, something inside of us feels entitled to happiness. If we believe the void of happiness can be filled by the five P's, we are heading for trouble. Feeling entitled to the five P's numbs our ability to appreciate the moment without judging it in terms of what we have and what we want. All of our attention is focused on future gains, and therefore we become unaware and unappreciative of the simple yet wondrous gifts that God has invested into the here and now—a breath of fresh air, health, a friend's smile. Unable to appreciate life as it is, we move further away from love and so also joy and gratitude. We have contracted leprosy of the spirit.

Furthermore, feeling entitled makes us unpleasant company. While focused on trying to obtain our perceived deserts, we fail to focus on the needs of others. We may be so absorbed by our own wants that we don't really see or hear others. Our emotional senses are numbed. Or, if we do concern ourselves with the needs of others, we do so in hopes of getting something in return—a little praise, a little sympathy, a little gain of some kind.

We may be easily offended. Not obtaining what we feel we deserve, we sink into a sulk, or we rage, or we retaliate, or we loudly broadcast the perceived injustice to all who have ears. In these ways we isolate ourselves. People avoid us. It is very difficult for people to deal with those who have no cares beyond their litany of complaints and injustices. But even if some people remain by our side, we aren't really connecting with them so long as we are plugged into our own entitlement. So feeling entitled, be it to material things, to social rewards, or to a different self, truly is like leprosy of the spirit—we are left unable to sense joy and we are left isolated.

If we are plagued with vague feelings of dull dissatisfaction or full-blown depression, a close examination will likely reveal a disconnection from God and others. We may find that we are hoping to fill the emotional void with the five P's, and so we are focusing on the future. In so doing, we fail to appreciate the blessings of the here and now. If this is the case, we can then realize that we are suffering from spiritual leprosy.

Jesus has the cure for our spiritual leprosy, and through this account he reaches out to us with his healing touch. The Samaritan returns to praise and thank Jesus. Jesus says, "Get up and go on your way; your faith has made you well." Just as faith in Jesus was critical for the Samaritan's healing, so it is for our own. Yet if we are to truly put our faith into Jesus, we must recall Jesus's fundamental nature, Divine Love. To put our faith in the true Jesus is to allow the precepts of Divine Love to rule our thoughts and actions to the best of our ability—that we lay down our lives for others, that we forgive all, that we be servants to the well-being of others even as Jesus was a servant to the well-being of all humanity.

The text mentions twice that of the ten, the only man to thank and praise Jesus was a foreigner, a Samaritan. This is significant. Unlike a citizen, automatically entitled to all the rights of the country, a foreigner does not expect such privileges. As in the previous healing, the message for our lives is that as we receive Jesus's healing and enter ever deeper into his kingdom, it is essential for us to remember that we are foreigners, guests. If we are given a taste of heaven while here on earth, it is not because we are deserving citizens, but because our Lord is gracious. This attitude can help dispel the sense of entitlement that diminishes our ability to feel joy.

It is remarkable how many of the major healings we've reviewed involve not Jews, but foreigners—the Canaanite woman and her daughter, the Centurion, and now this Samaritan man. It is easier to be grateful to God and love God when we know the grace we receive is a merciful gift that we do not rightly deserve. When we forget our rightful position as a servant, we begin to feel entitled. We focus on what we need and want. And this focus on the self eliminates our possibility of feeling the peace and joy of selfless love.

We are servants to the community of humanity. Rather than an individualistic vision of reality that gives rise to the pursuit of the five P's, the Lord of Love awakens us to our inherent unity with all humanity. The Lord of Love motivates us to seek the well-being of all we encounter. We begin to awaken to our true joy.

Most of us, at some point in our lives, spend some time in emotional drought. We simply don't feel joy. Perhaps the day-in, day-out routine of our lives feels mechanical and meaningless. Maybe our personal relationships seem dull and old. For some of us, this joyless state can last years, even a lifetime. The good news is that Jesus has the remedy to restore joy to our lives. This healing account is about gratitude.

When we feel dead to the world, isolated and numb, we can receive Jesus's healing by mirroring the actions of the Samaritan. We can get on our knees and thank Jesus. We can praise God with a loud voice for his overwhelming graciousness. Once we begin thanking him, we'll soon see that there are not enough hours in a day to contain the thanks he deserves. Think of all we have been given! The very air that sustains us; the mournful beauty of a dove's song; the spectacular, ever-changing canvas of the sky; the smiles of children; the love of a friend; the roof above us; the spiritual life we receive from God; rain on the windowpane; a pet cat; the Word of God through which we learn about and enter into relationship with our Lord. There is an infinite amount of thanks and praise we can give to Jesus, our Lord and God.

Even when we are numbed with depression or a sense of entitlement, we can force ourselves to kneel. We can force the mouth to pronounce thanks. We can do this every day. The miracle, of course, is that by going through these motions of gratitude, Jesus will begin to instill genuine gratitude into our hearts and minds. With the increasing sense of gratitude comes an increasing sense of joy. What at first felt like hollow lip service becomes filled with genuine depth and feeling. To help this occur, we must remember that in truth, we are undeserving citizens of God's kingdom. We are foreigners, very fortunate to have been given the chance to live at all! As Dr. Seuss puts it in *Happy Birthday to You!* (1959): "Shout loud, 'I am lucky to be what I am! Thank goodness I'm not just a clam or a ham or a dusty old jar of sour gooseberry jam!'"

There are three critical elements in our healing from depression. The first is that we learn to spot our imagined entitlement to the pursuit of the five P's. The second is to understand this entitlement as an indicator that we have fallen into the delusion of individual materialism and, accordingly, reorient ourselves to our true purpose, love for the well-being of all humanity. Finally, with a new orientation, we become willing to surrender those feelings to God and replace them with praise and gratitude. The mind abhors a vacuum. We cannot simply oust thoughts of entitlement without replacing them with an alternative. Praise is the alternative that Jesus prescribes in this healing.

Praise is a wonderful antidepressant. The more we practice, the more we feel the urge to praise. It is a positive, upward cycle of joy. When we feel unhappy, let that be a signal that it is time to praise and thank God for the incredible bounty we all have already been given. No matter what situation we may be facing; no matter what our life condition may be, there is room and time for praise.

Conversely, no matter how much we have, there will still be room for us to covet more. Dissatisfaction isn't caused by lack; on the contrary, perceived lack is caused by dissatisfaction. We meet trouble when we attempt to obtain joy through temporal phenomena and physical things. The very nature of the natural world causes these pleasures to fade with time, and so the more we gain, the more we feel desperate dissatisfaction. Each time we reach out for more possessions, more achievements, more gratifications, the pleasure is a little less novel, a little more routine. We may feel the solution is to obtain better quality, more quantity, and different varieties. But no amount, no variety, and no quality of what the material world has to offer can fill the spiritual emptiness inside. What we really need is a connection with the Lord of Love. Gratitude and praise can forge the connection.

Once awakened to our connection with the Lord of Love, we will in turn awaken to our connection with all of humanity. Within this state of heightened spiritual awareness, unhappiness and dissatisfaction fade to nothing. Selfish motivations slip away and are replaced with the joyful desire to bless others.

The very attempt to gain material rewards for ourselves is exactly what shuts us off from the true reward that satisfies, the joy of spirit. Spiritual joy is all around us and within each moment. Joy is an intrinsic part of reality. I truly believe that it is a part of the fundamental fabric of life. God is the author of joy, and so joy is part of his being. He is omnipresent, therefore so is his joy. In the final analysis, life is joy. It must be so, since the Lord of Love authored life.

I live in Nepal. It is a Himalayan land of great mystery, majesty, and beauty. It is also a land of great poverty. An amazing and admirable quality of many Nepali people is their warm hospitality and friendliness. People who have very few material possessions beam with the most genuine smiles. They are ready to share their meager possessions with strangers. Despite their hardships, they haven't forgotten how to be happy. In fact, the more rural and economically poor the area, the more rich with joy the people seem to be. Nepali culture is a collectivistic culture in which people are more sensitive to the inherent connection between all people. These beautiful people have taught me the important lesson that joy and contentment do not depend on the things of this world or in "grand" achievements, but on the unity of Love.

When we think of miraculous healings of leprosy, we may recall the story of Naaman and Elisha (2 Kings 5). Naaman is the commander of the powerful army of Aram. He has all he could wish for: power, position, possessions, and pleasures in plenty. But he also suffers from leprosy. One of his servants, a young girl from Israel, suggests to Naaman that he visit Elisha, the great prophet of Israel. At first his pride stops him from following the suggestion of a servant girl. But, perhaps in desperation, he eventually journeys to Elisha's home with an immense amount of gold, silver, and other treasures for Elisha.

Before Naaman arrives, Elisha sends his servant, Gehazi, with a message for Naaman: the commander is to wash seven times in the Jordan and he will be healed of leprosy. Naaman flies into a rage because Elisha didn't even bother to meet him. He had wanted some big ceremony. His dignity had been slighted. "Are not Abana and Pharpar, the rivers of Damascus, better than all the waters of Israel? Could I not wash in them, and be clean?" he spits out with fury.

But again the servants help Naaman by urging him to at least try the suggestion of the prophet. And in doing so, Naaman is healed so that his flesh is like that "of a child." With great gratitude and joy, he returns to Elisha to offer thanks as well as the great wealth he had brought, saying, "Now I know that there is no God in all the earth except in Israel; please accept a present from your servant." But Elisha responds by saying, "As the Lord lives, whom I serve, I will receive nothing."

Naaman therefore begs that he be allowed to take two mule-loads of Israeli earth back to Syria "for your servant will no longer offer burnt offering or sacrifice to any god except the Lord." Elisha grants Naaman's wish. But Elisha's greedy servant Gehazi is upset with his master for refusing the fortune that Naaman had wanted to give for the healing. Catching up to Naaman, Gehazi lies, saying that some sons of the prophets had arrived and that Elisha now needed some silver and clothes for them. Naaman eagerly gives the silver and clothes. On returning, Elisha asks Gehazi where he had been. Gehazi again lies, saying that he had not gone anywhere. Elisha responds, "Did I not go with you in spirit when someone left his chariot to meet you? Is this a time to accept money and to accept clothing, olive orchards and vineyards, sheep and oxen, and male and female slaves? Therefore the leprosy of Naaman shall cling to you, and to your descendants forever." And indeed, Gehazi left Elisha leprous, "as white as snow."

We see within this story the same message we see in the healing of the ten lepers. Before, Naaman had an arrogant, entitled attitude.

He felt entitled to dignity and pomp. Elisha should have come and met him, he thought. But when he was willing to listen to the voices of mere servants and so gained humility, he was cured of leprosy. Naaman learned that the Lord and the Lord alone is God. The name of the Lord as written in the Old Testament is Yahweh, which means He Who Is Existence, or we might say *reality* or *life*. If we want to love Yahweh, we need to love the here and now—existence as it is. We need to love life on life's terms.

But in his heart Gehazi worshiped a false god, material wealth. He felt entitled to the wealth of Naaman. Gehazi's greed caused him to become leprous. The same is true for us. If we set selfish gain as the goal of our heart, it will lead us to an ever-decreasing sense of joy. We become spiritually leprous. Dissatisfaction with our share of worldly possessions, position, prestige, power, and pleasure will cause us to ever seek more and desire more. We will never know satisfaction. But by coming to seek only God and his will, we will be healed.

After his healing, Naaman's flesh became like that of a "little child." Jesus says that only those who become like little children shall know heaven. My wife and I have been given the joy of caring for many children. Little children marvel and take the greatest joy in the simplest of things. The joy they feel is communicated to all around them. This joy, the joy of gratitude and delight in the simple things of life, is what Jesus wants for us. And indeed, we need it if we want to enter into his kingdom, his joy.

Naaman at first felt entitled to a meeting with Elisha and a grand ceremony of healing, but he changed and became humble. In the end, all Namaan needed to be happy were two heaps of dirt so that he could worship. When our hearts become accustomed to expressing humble gratitude as a foreigner allowed to dwell within God's kingdom of mercy, we'll be overjoyed with the simplest of things.

To continue on the path of spiritual development, we must foster a humble attitude of gratitude. Without gratitude, any healing we may have felt so far will fade away. Feelings of entitlement make us feel that our plans for life are superior to God's plan, which is reality. We believe we deserve more than what God provides. We, like Gehazi, have set ourselves over and above our Master. We try to steal for ourselves that which we imagine we deserve. All we succeed in obtaining is spiritual leprosy.

After we begin the work of spiritual development, we may enter a phase of discontented boredom. We miss our old way of life. We're doing what we know we *should* do, but we aren't happy and we feel deprived. We've sacrificed a lot; we're putting in a lot of work, and we feel entitled to some rewards. We may feel that we have to get some joy in our lives. Praising God fills our spiritual need for joy.

We need not limit our praise to set times. We can offer quiet thanks and praise spontaneously throughout the flow of our days. We can take a moment to notice the details of this amazing gift called life. Just today, as I was walking down a familiar road, I noticed my thoughts were distracted with worries and ambitions. I switched gears and just began thinking, "thank you." Suddenly, I noticed the swallows darting all around me with astounding agility. It brought an instant smile to my face. They had been there all along. God had been hoping I'd see them so that he could bring me a smile, but I couldn't see them until I changed my mindset. It's the difference between "I want . . ." and "thanks." "I want" focuses the mind on what we do not have and what isn't here. "Thanks" focuses us on the overflowing blessings that are all around us all the time here and now.

There is another important point to be made within this miracle. The text says that the Samaritan returned praising and thanking God "with a loud voice." This is important. In our modern society, many of us are unaccustomed to and therefore uncomfortable with praising God out loud. But why not try? What, really, do we have to lose? Nothing, of course; and we have everything to gain. After having looked at this miracle in depth, begin praising God out loud, even if it is in private. The results are undeniable. Happiness and gratitude increase. Gratitude to the Lord is a choice and a practice, and the gift of joy is the result.

Even if we do not suffer from depression ourselves, we are likely still a part of the problematically individualistic and materialistic society. We thus still have some homework. Despite the traditional ostracism of lepers, it ironically turns out that leprosy is not a very contagious disease. Ninety-five percent of humanity is immune. It is also true that simple massage therapy can prevent the disease from causing deformities. Since we know the cure for spiritual leprosy, we can afford to reach out to those around us who suffer. There is a natural tendency to avoid those who are depressed. Yet if we remain present with them, maybe even offering extra attention—the emotional equivalent of a massage—we likely will be aiding in their recovery. We will be living out the healing truth spoken in this miracle: our true purpose is to be humble servants lovingly serving the well-being and unity of humanity. There is no higher form of praise and gratitude to the Lord of Love than service to our fellow human beings.

MEDITATION

After arriving into a meditative state of mind, put yourself as vividly as possible in the place of one leper among nine others in ancient Israel. Feel the loneliness and pain of isolation from your loved ones. Feel the sensation of being diseased, feared, and loathsome. Experience the feelings of hopelessness at ever being healed. Allow yourself to really get in touch with these depressive feelings. Now you see Jesus walking nearby. You cry out for help and he responds! You are told to go to the priest and so you do. But on the way, you find yourself healed. You are overjoyed. Feel that ecstasy! You run back to Jesus and worship him with a loud voice of praise. You feel his hand on your back. It is the first time anyone has touched you in years. You grab his hand and hold it in yours. He doesn't recoil. He simply smiles at you and says, "Were there not ten made clean? But the other nine, where are they? Was none of them found to return and give praise to God except this foreigner? Get up, and go on your way; your faith has made you well."

Now praise God.

LEAVES

1. Long-term discontent and depression can be thought of as leprosy of the spirit.

2. This spiritual leprosy, i.e., dissatisfaction, is caused by feelings of entitlement.

3. Dissatisfaction is not cured, only aggravated, by acquiring what is desired.

4. True happiness is obtained by fostering gratitude.

5. Praising and thanking God on a regular basis is the best way of fostering gratitude.

6. Our culture is largely based on an individualistic materialism that gives rise to spiritual leprosy. Focusing on the unity and well-being of all humanity is a part of our cure.

FRUIT

1. Every other day set time aside to praise God vocally, loudly. Thank him and mention specific things for which you are grateful. On the alternate days, sing praise songs to the Lord.

2. From time to time throughout each day, and whenever you feel dissatisfied, stop and offer praise and thanks to God in your heart.

3. Focus on the gifts of each moment.

4. Write a gratitude list.

5. Try to make praise and thanks to God the underlying mantra of your heart, the all-encompassing atmosphere of your mind from which your thoughts arise.

6. Make it a point to serve others in some way each day.

1. If you suffer from depression, did you feel less depressed this week?

2. Did you find the meditation helpful? What insights (emotional or mental) did you gain from it?

3. How did you find praising God vocally? How long did it take to stop feeling silly in doing so?

4. Did you find that vocal praise made you feel happier?

5. What did you write on your gratitude list?

6. If you had an increase in gratitude and praise this week, how did it affect your interactions?

7. What effect did your acts of service have on you?

9

HEALING FROM FEAR

"Am I not to drink the cup that the Father has given me?"

Matthew 26:51–54

Suddenly, one of those with Jesus put his hand on his sword, drew it, and struck the slave of the high priest, cutting off his ear. Then Jesus said to him, "Put your sword back in its place; for all who take the sword will perish by the sword. Do you think that I cannot appeal to my Father, and he will at once send me more than twelve legions of angels? But how then would the scriptures be fulfilled, which say it must happen this way?"

Mark 14:46–52

Then they laid their hands on him and arrested him. But one of those who stood near drew his sword and struck the slave of the high priest, cutting off his ear. Then Jesus said to them, "Have you come out with swords and clubs to arrest me as though I were a bandit? Day after day I was with you in the temple teaching, and you did not arrest me. But let the scriptures be fulfilled." All of them deserted him and fled. A certain young man was following him, wearing nothing but a linen cloth. They caught hold of him, but he left the linen cloth and ran off naked.

Luke 22:49–51

When those who were around him saw what was coming, they asked, "Lord, should we strike with the sword?" Then one of them struck the slave of the high priest and cut off his right ear. But Jesus said, "No more of this!" And he touched the ear and healed him.

John 18:10–11

Then Simon Peter, who had a sword, drew it, struck the high priest's slave, and cut off his right ear. The slave's name was Malchus. Jesus said to Peter, "Put your sword back into its sheath. Am I not to drink the cup that the Father has given me?"

~~~

I believe that held within the account of this healing is one of the most profound curative lessons that we can receive. This miracle shows us how to allow God to remove fear from our lives, leaving us with a purer and gentler relationship with life. Having talked with many people who actively seek to allow God to evolve them spiritually, it seems that we humans share in common a deep-seated, underlying fear that taints most everything we do. In fact, everyone I've listened to on this matter states that their addictions, resentments, and problems are, as far as they can see, fueled by fear. This fear takes on various manifestations. Losing face, psychological vulnerability, financial insecurity, loneliness, death, condemnation—the list is long. But all these fears stem from a single, underlying source: the sense of self. The self worries about itself. To have our consciousness raised to a plane higher than that of the self is to be released from most, if not all, of our perceived problems. By means of this miracle, the Lord shows us how to transcend our selves and so our fears.

This is a miracle different from all others offered in the Old and New Testaments in that the injury that is healed is a battle wound. One man, Peter, actively sought to injure another, Malchus.

Each of the four gospels describes this incident, and each adds slightly different details. In Matthew we read Jesus's words about angels. In Mark, we read about a young man who flees. Luke is the only gospel that reveals the fact that Jesus healed the ear after it was sliced off. John is where we find out the names of the people involved, Peter and Malchus. Each detail is important, and taken together they increase our ability to sense God's healing and power in this event.

To better understand the message of this healing, it helps to understand Peter's personality. Peter's character is clearly revealed by looking at his words and deeds throughout the four Gospels. He is a man of great activity and passion. He very much loves the Lord and wants to be a good servant to him. Peter's eager passion for the Lord is demonstrated when he takes a few steps on the water, believing in Jesus's power to keep him from sinking. After the resurrection, Peter runs and is the first to enter the empty tomb. A few days later, while fishing, Peter is so happy to see the Lord that he jumps out of the boat and swims ashore.

Yet Peter's passion is consistently misguided. Peter abhors the idea of Jesus encountering anything painful or base. In one of their first interactions Peter says to the Lord, "Go away from me, Lord, for I am a sinful man" (Luke 5:8). Similarly, Peter initially refuses to let Jesus wash his feet. Loathing the topic, Peter reprimands Jesus for speaking of his eventual death. Jesus, however, refuses to let any self-concern hinder his goal of offering his love freely to Peter and the whole human race. In each of these cases, Peter's idea of how to love Jesus was off the mark. In each case, Jesus had to educate Peter about what was necessary for their relationship. Jesus *did not* leave him, though Peter was sinful. Jesus severely rebuked Peter for contradicting the truth that Jesus would die as he predicted. Jesus *did* wash Peter's feet, despite Peter's reluctance.

Here in this scene we see the exact same dynamic at work. The moment is very dramatic as the high priests with their armed mob arrive in the dark of night to capture and kill Jesus. We can sympathize with Peter's desperate attempt to save his Lord from the evil intent of these men. Jesus is in danger. Just hours before, Peter claimed in earnest belief that he would sooner die or be imprisoned than deny Jesus. Peter rushes to protect Jesus with violence, but in so doing, acts completely opposite to the will of God. And as Jesus had predicted, despite Peter's zealous love for Jesus, he denies him, not once, but three times that very night. Well before the verbal denial during the trial, Peter's initial abandonment of Jesus begins here, with the account of the arrest.

Time and again Jesus taught nonviolence: "Turn the other cheek . . . love your enemy . . . do good to those who hurt you." The act of striking another human being with a sword is contrary to the essence of Jesus's teaching. It shows that even in this late hour, Peter still didn't understand the heart and message of Jesus. Peter is still trusting his own ideas over and above Jesus's. He is gripped by a fear that Jesus's true message of love and nonviolence cannot succeed. Jesus said many times in various ways that it was necessary for him to be taken, tried, and killed. Peter just couldn't accept this truth. He also fails to realize that were it Jesus's will, Jesus could easily evade or counter the attack by means of his angels, as is mentioned in Matthew.

The crux of the problem in Peter's walk with God was that he mixed his own ideas and expectations with his faith in Jesus. Rather than trusting in God's will, Peter trusted in his idea of God's will. When things seemed to be going Peter's way in relation to Jesus, he was very enthusiastic in faith. When events didn't go as Peter wanted and expected, his faith wavered. He experienced fear. Like Peter, when things are going contrary to how we imagine they should go, we become afraid. Fear arises when our wants and expectations aren't met.

All of us who embark on the journey of becoming truly loving people spend time in a Peter-like stage of faith. We love God intensely, but part of our love is wrapped up in the hope that God is going to make things go according to our desire and our plan. We think that we know what is good and best for us, our partner, the kids, the boss, the community, the church, and the world around us. We think we know what God should do. But rarely does life unfold as we expect and hope, and when we are disappointed, we tend to get scared and angry. We may, like Peter, turn our back on God. In fact, the feelings of fear indicate that to some extent we already have turned our faith away from God in favor of our own plans and strength.

To trust God completely means we know that everything is going as he sees best, regardless of how it appears to us, and regardless of how it matches what we want or expect. When we enter this state of mind, we come to know true peace—peace not of this world, but the peace of our Lord.

Peter believed, but the Jesus he believed in was different than the real Jesus. And in the Garden of Gethsemane at the time of the arrest the discrepancy between Peter's imagined Jesus and the real Jesus became evident. Peter fled and denied the real Jesus. Peter was still holding onto the Jesus of his imagination—the one that would not be arrested; the one that would rise up and rule Israel as an earthly king. Early in our walk, we may find ourselves denying Jesus in a similar manner when things don't turn out as we had imagined and prayed. We don't get the job. Our partner leaves us. A loved one dies. But the message embedded within this miracle can heal and correct our faith in a way that allows us to stay with Jesus and receive his comfort regardless of our own will and of how life unfolds.

Now let's turn to the high priest and his servant, whose ear Peter severed. They were marching through the night on what they considered a mission of paramount importance—to capture and deal with this scoundrel named Jesus. Jesus was a major threat to them in more than one way. Jesus refused to conform to the rules of the Sabbath. And as a very public and popular figure, his actions threatened to undermine the whole Jewish way of life and religious code. People were likely to follow his example in breaking the rules Moses had taught. The Jewish religion was very legalistic. Obeying the law was of paramount importance.

But more disturbing to the priests, scribes, Pharisees, and other religious authorities was the fact that Jesus claimed to be the Son of

God. He even equated himself with Yahweh by saying such things as, "Before Abraham was, I am" (John 8:58) and "The Father and I are one" (John 10:30). In Israelite tradition, the name Yahweh was so holy that they would neither write nor speak that name. How dare this man, whom they considered a mere mortal, equate himself with holiness so perfect that it can't be mentioned by name? This self-proclaimed Messiah didn't fit into the accepted paradigm of what the Messiah would be. In previous chapters we have already seen why the scribes and other leaders of the Jewish nation would have had such a hard time changing their ideas about the coming Savior. They were experts of the Law of Moses.

But apart from being a religious threat, they also judged Jesus to be a political threat. Many of Jesus's followers were expecting Jesus to oust the Romans and restore Israel as an independent nation of God's special and chosen people. The priests feared that Jesus would attempt a political revolution against the Romans. They didn't believe Jesus was divine, and they didn't believe that a political coup led by him would succeed in anything except inciting a devastating backlash from Rome. We see this fact in the following discourse held among the religious leaders: "'What are we to do? This man is performing many signs. If we let him go on like this, everyone will believe in him, and the Romans will come and destroy both our holy place and our nation.' But one of them, Caiaphas, said to them, 'You know nothing at all! You do not understand that it is better for you to have one man die for the people than to have the whole nation destroyed'" (John 11:47–50).

Until then, Rome had afforded Israel a great deal of autonomy. Rome permitted the Jews to worship as they liked in the temple of their tradition. Jewish priests, scribes, and leaders still enjoyed a great deal of power. But if Rome perceived that the current system was resulting only in upheaval and attacks against Rome, their lenient attitude would come to an end. Jewish power would be dissolved, and using martial law, Rome would impose its own system upon the land. Roman religion would be enforced. The priests and scribes would be stripped of their power and position. Jewish rules would be replaced by Roman rules; Jewish rulers with Roman rulers. And likely the Romans would separate the people—importing many foreigners to occupy Israel and forcing many Jews to leave and settle in other parts of the empire. In fact, this is exactly what happened a few decades later in 70 AD.

So the rulers of the Jewish nation feared Jesus as a threat to everything they believed to be holy, good, and right. He was a threat to Jewish religion and the Jewish state. In capturing Jesus, they believed that they were serving God's purposes. They would save the people from a deluded teacher and a diluted form of the Mosaic law. They would save the nation from political overthrow. In their minds, to capture and kill Jesus was just and good. It was necessary to protect and preserve the Jewish religion and state.

In other words, they were just like Peter. They were motivated in exactly the same way that Peter was motivated when he cut off the ear of their servant. From a sense of fear, both Peter and the ruling Jews wanted desperately to defend what they believed to be true and good. Both were willing to use violence to protect their misguided conceptions of God's will. Both Peter and the ruling Jews loved not so much God, but their imagined notions of God. But both were unable to see that they were worshiping, loving, and trying to defend a false idea of God, a false idol constructed from their thoughts. Both sides adamantly believed that their misconception of God was the true God, and both were filled with fear.

So when Peter sliced off Malchus's ear, in a sense, he was attacking the very image of himself. Peter's act of cutting off Malchus's ear simultaneously was an act of cutting himself off from the true Jesus, our spiritual King. Interestingly, the name Malchus means *king*. And those who tried to cut Jesus off from life didn't realize that this attempt would actually cut themselves off from the source of life—Jesus. The ear that fell is an image of Peter slicing himself from the Lord. It is an image of those who, in crucifying Jesus, cut themselves off from the Lord.

But more poignantly, the severed ear is an image of ourselves when we lose track of the real God while pursuing our deluded ideas of who God is. When we attack others from a sense of faith, we cut ourselves off from the true and living Lord of Love. God is love, and when we act contrary to love, we are severed from God. When God is separated from us, it isn't God who dies, but we—just as it is the ear that will perish, and not the man, when the two are separated. Jesus's reattaching the ear to Malchus's body foreshadows the resurrection of Jesus and of our own restoration to life. His death was actually ours, the human race's. Our attempt to subjugate Love to our self-based will only succeeds in causing our own spiritual death. His resurrection was actually our resurrection effected by the fact that the Lord of Love continued to love us despite our spiritual insanity.

People of different faiths clash in violence, vehemently believing they are fighting for the sake of God and by God's power. Even people of different sects within the same faith frequently grow hostile and intolerant of one another. The same kinds of conflict that arise between nations and groups of people also arise between us as individuals. Violence, be it emotional or physical, arises from an underlying fear. Peter feared for the future of Jesus, himself, and the nation. The high priest and others who came to capture Jesus were likewise motivated by a fear for Yahweh, themselves, and the future of the nation.

Whenever we find ourselves clashing with others, we can know for sure that we are worshiping the wrong God—one that gives rise to fear. The clash itself reveals that our understanding of God is flawed. God does not wish that we attack one another in an attempt to "defend" our rightness or his. As he says, he could win any war with his angels if that were his desire. God's true will (as expressed in his commandments to us) is that we love one another as he has loved us, that we lay down our lives for each other. In attacking, we attack both ourselves and our God. What we do to one another, we do to him, for he is present within all of us. And if we clash with others, we can know that we are in fact severing ourselves from God and the communion of human beings, God's body. This body is bound together by means of love and desire to serve, just as the cells of the body are united in useful service to the greater whole.

The same conflicts that arise between nations, or individuals, also arise within corresponding facets of our own being. We grow weary, or angry, or even hateful with our own being. At heart, we are very afraid that we cannot be healed. As we trudge the road of spiritual development we often place faith in the goal but forget to have faith in the process. Like Peter, we adore the idea of an idyllic end, but abhor the necessary ups and downs along the way. We forget that God is not only the God of outcomes, but also of processes. He is in charge of our lives on both the good days and the bad days. What we see as failure in God's plan is a learning experience.

The healing essence here is this: we can keep trusting God no matter what happens around us or within us. The disciple John exemplifies this kind of trust. While all the disciples forsook Jesus and Peter denied him three times, John fearlessly entered into the inner chamber of the court of Jesus's trial. He remained present despite the fear and danger.

When we get upset because things don't go according to our wishes, we can even practice thanking God for this as a lesson in deepening our trust in the true Jesus. The pathways of our life are guided by him. He sees if we need uplifting. He knows if we need humbling. He knows if we need to remain passive or if we need to take action. We can trust that he is leading us and all others perfectly through life. Rather than trusting in our plans and goals, we can trust that the process of life as it unfolds is God's plan. God is pure love, pure wisdom, and pure power. What is there to worry about? If we grow upset with ourselves and our shortcomings, it is good to remember that God made us. If we grow upset when people attack or hurt us, we can consider this a chance to practice and grow in love. If we grow weary of the state of the world, we can remember Jesus's advice to consider the birds of the air and the flowers of the field.

Christianity is supremely simple—we are to love one another as Jesus loved us. That is all there is to it. To the extent that we do this, we are integrated into the body of God and the fellowship of human beings. To the extent we neglect to obey the New Commandment, we sever ourselves from the vine, from the body of Christ. Christianity is simple in thought, but extremely difficult in practice. It is a goal that we can never fully achieve. We can grow better at this selfless love for eternity. The miracle offered here is not instant freedom from selfishness and the fear it entails. Rather, it is revealing to us the way of progressive freedom from self-based fear.

In fact, patience is a central element of the healing. We can remain calm despite the imperfections we see within ourselves, in others, and in the world, knowing that God's plan unfolds mysteriously over time. Salvation doesn't happen overnight. Just knowing that we aren't going to be instantly free from fear and selfishness goes a long way in reducing our fears and selfishness! It's OK if we aren't perfect, or if we stumble on the way. It is all part of God's plan. "Put your sword back into its sheath. Am I not to drink the cup that the Father has given me?" When Peter attacked the high priest's servant, he was attacking himself. We don't need to attack ourselves any longer.

It is love that counts. Love is the Lord's central, eternal command, and love is at the heart of all he did. In the parable of the Good Samaritan, Jesus showed us that righteousness is proved not by declared faith, but by love made real in action (Luke 10:29–37). When confronted with a sinful woman Jesus said, "Therefore I tell you, her sins, which were many, have been forgiven; hence she has shown great love. But the one to whom little is forgiven, loves little" (Luke 7:47). Jesus said, "Each tree is known by its own fruit" (Luke 6:44); "unless you repent, you will all perish" (Luke 13:5); and, in a parable, "If [the tree] bears fruit next year, well and good; but if not, you can cut it down" (Luke 13:9). In the parable of the two sons (Matt. 21:28–31), one says he will not work, but, regretting it, goes to work; the other says he will, but does not. Jesus says the first is of the kind who enter heaven. And in Jesus's description of the coming of the Son of Man, it is the sheep, those who have loved in deed, that are saved (Matt. 25:31–46).

All of this is to say that faith is the servant of love. When we think love is the servant of faith, we, like Malchus and Peter, can't help but end up in conflict. We sacrifice love in our attempt to defend faith. Jesus is love, so it is the Lord that we sacrifice.

Wonderfully, love is limitless. There are no restraints on who we may love. Nor is there any limit to how much we can grow in love. We can love forever more deeply. Loving is where we are truly free. The more we love, the more life we receive from Jesus. He is the very love we feel and act on. The more we practice love, the more adept we will become, and the greater the depth of love we will feel. At first, we force ourselves to love, but in the end, we can't stop ourselves from loving. That is the life of Jesus growing in us and filling us with the joy and peace he has promised to us.

A mentor of mine often says, "I can be right, or I can be happy." When faced with trials and troubles our instinctual reaction is fear. Our self-based sense of what should happen is threatened. If we insist on being right, it won't be long before we become argumentative and self-righteousness. Rather than trying to prove we are in the right, we can love and serve. Even if others are argumentative and combative with us, we can still choose to respond with love. We will find that in doing so we enter peace and happiness.

Another friend of mine once backed out of a blind driveway and ran into the van of an elderly lady. My friend was clearly in the wrong. However, this lady came running out of her car, flung open the door of my friend's SUV and said, "I love you! Are you OK?" She was a very devout Christian, and from this incident it seems that she well understood Jesus's message. She didn't care about who was right. She was not interested in defending her rightness. She just loved people, and so love is what flowed out of her mouth and deeds.

When I was a freshman in college, my roommate had a pet iguana. To my displeasure, the iguana was given full access to the room. It wasn't long before he discovered the mirror at the top of my clothes cabinet. Every day I would come back to find my belongings strewn across the floor and an angry lizard at war with the image in the mirror. After a while I insisted that the reptile remain in its cage while not supervised.

But the image of this iguana attacking its own reflection left an impression on me. It is a perfect illustration of what we are like when we value ideas and plans over love. We get worked up defending this or that idea, against imagined enemies; but the only real enemy is our self-based mistaken values. Sometimes we attack verbally, physically, or even just in our thoughts, anything that seems to threaten us. This might be another person or ideology, but more often it is circumstances or our own failures. Our failure to improve spiritually causes us fear, and from that fear we attack ourselves. Our faith that Jesus can save us from our personal hell wavers like Peter's at the trial. Circumstances go terribly wrong—completely contrary to what we had hoped, worked, and planned for. We get angry at reality for not going our way. Our faith that God loves us wavers. We are stuck in fear and act from fear.

But all of this is delusion. The enemy isn't real. The perceived enemy is a reflection of our own delusion and fear. I once had a powerful dream in which I was in the midst of chaotic jungle warfare. Warplanes were screaming overhead, and there was a pervading sense of doom all around. As I was running, I came to a clearing. In the midst of the clearing, a book was lying open atop a large rock. As I approached, I saw that the book was luminous with a shimmering golden light. I looked into the book and saw just one glowing letter, the Hebrew letter He. I instantly understood that there was no enemy at all. Caught in thick confusion, we were fighting ourselves.

Love has no real enemy because Love loves all. No matter what happens, no matter how we fail, no matter what others say or do, we can trust the Lord of Love, and so continue to give love. Jesus put the ear back on Malchus. He forgave those who attacked and killed him. Such is the nature of Divine Love. And such is the face of living and true faith.

We sometimes say to our children, "Do you hear me?" In this question, we are actually commanding compliance to our will. We also sometimes say, "I hear you!" to express sympathy for a friend's plight. Even in colloquial language, the ear is associated with congruence of the will. Jesus's rejoining the ear back onto Malchus represents the fact that Love is able to reincorporate our errant will back into congruence with the one true will, that of Love.

In the Gospel of Mark, we read about a man who flees the scene, leaving his garment in the hands of those who are grasping at him. Humor me as I delve into some imaginative speculation. Could it be that this young man is Malchus, the high priest's servant? Having received this healing, he is convinced of Jesus's innocence and goodness. He can no longer serve the high priest. As he tries to run, the officers of the high priest grab at him, but, unwilling to remain with those who wish to kill Jesus—the amazing man who touched and healed him—he parts with his clothes and runs away naked into the night. Just as he is stripped of his clothing, he is also stripped of all his previous conceptions of right, wrong, and who the Lord is.

He has much to think about. It would seem likely that he would later seek out the disciples to find out more about the one who healed him, and in so doing forgave him. Just as Saul would later change his name to Paul when he became a follower of Jesus, perhaps this man, Malchus, changes his name after he joins the disciples. I like to imagine that he changes it from Malchus to Marcus. He is soon the right-hand man of Simon Peter, the one who had struck him. He records the words of Peter into what becomes known as the Gospel of Mark (Marcus). This is why he alone writes about the young man who fled in the Garden of Gethsemane. He would spend the rest of his life assisting Peter on many adventures and travels, all to spread the amazing news—that God manifested himself on earth so that all might be saved, which is to say spiritually healed. And his message is that we love one another.

The two enemies, Peter and Malchus, are now one united force for good. And it is love, Jesus's love, that forged the union. Both had been blind and in service to a false god. But Jesus's love opened their eyes to reality and opened their hearts to love. It is from this love that they join as fast friends. This is speculation, of course, but I enjoy thinking of it this way. Jesus's love is reality, and it alone unites humankind.

So in summary, the healing is twofold. First, we learn to trust in God regardless of what may be happening. The lesson is to let go of fear altogether. The second aspect of the healing is to come to know the real Lord Jesus: he who commands that we love one another as he loves us. In practicing love, we are united in the body of Christ.

MEDITATIONS

1. After entering a meditative state of mind, put yourself into the life of Malchus, the servant of the high priest. Feel the sense of adrenaline and righteousness as you go to bring justice to the troublemaker who stands to bring political and religious ruin to your country; the troublemaker who does away with tradition and the Sabbath rules, and who claims to be God. Allow yourself to feel that righteous zeal. You see the man named Judas kiss him, the sign. *Finally, the madness shall end,* you think as you rush closer. Suddenly you see one of Jesus's disciples pull out a sword and raise his arms. You feel the blade on your skin as he slices off your ear. The pain is intense, and you feel the hot, thick blood spilling onto your shoulder and running down your leg. You are filled with a mix of fear, rage, and disbelief. You are right next to the man named Jesus when you bend down to look for your ear. He bends down, too, and says, "No more of this!" In the darkness, he picks something up and touches it to your head. In that instant, all feelings of rage and fear and righteous zeal evaporate as the warmth of utter peace and acceptance flows through your body from the spot where he healed your ear. You breathe in deeply, and the night air is cool and fresh. You suddenly remember why you have come, and are stuck aghast at the idea of hurting this man Jesus whose love has healed you and

transformed you. You try to run away, but others of the mob clutch at your clothes. You'd rather run naked and ashamed than continue to be associated with those who wish to kill Jesus. You run down into the wooded slope. You feel as if you have just been born.

2. Meditate on the fact that life is the ever-unfolding revelation of Divine Love, and the fact that we can rest calm and peaceful in the process, even when we don't know what the heck is going on, or why.

3. In a meditative state, go back and relive the above scene from Peter's perspective. Feel the fear, anger, and desperation as the guards come to arrest your beloved teacher. Watch yourself cut off Malchus's ear. How do you feel? Jesus bends down and picks up the ear, healing the wound. Suddenly, everything he has been trying to teach you becomes clear. Feel his love even as you watch the guards take him away.

LEAVES

1. Fear arises when we trust in our plans and ideas over and above God's reality.

2. Fear gives rise to conflict.

3. We can trust in God no matter what is happening within us or around us.

4. When things don't go our way, we can see it as a learning experience from God.

5. Faith is the servant of love.

FRUIT

1. Make time, about ten minutes, to meditate on the fact that God is Love, God is Wisdom, and God is Power.

2. When we sense any fear or combativeness, it is a sign that we need to pray: "Lord, I believe; help my disbelief that you are in this situation and taking care of things as is best in terms of eternity."

3. Next we turn to God with thanks, recalling that all events are

in his hands and the outcome will be for good regardless of how the circumstances look to us.

4. When we feel the urge to attack or to prove our rightness, we instead turn to our perceived enemy with a spirit of love. How can we bless the other?

DISCUSSION QUESTIONS

1. What was your experience of the first meditation?

2. What was your experience of the daily meditation?

3. Did you notice any changes in your daily routine as a result of the meditation?

4. Did you resolve any conflict or upset in a way that surprised you or was more productive than you had anticipated?

5. Did you feel more peace this week?

6. Can you think of a time when you blamed God because things didn't go your way?

7. Can you identify fear underneath this blame? What was it that made you afraid?

8. Do you find it difficult to bless those who have wronged you? What do you feel when you try?

9. In Malchus's position, could you forgive Peter for cutting off your ear?

10

HEALING FROM SPIRITUAL APATHY

"Take up your mat and walk."

John 5:1–14

After this there was a festival of the Jews, and Jesus went up to Jerusalem. Now in Jerusalem by the Sheep Gate there is a pool, called in Hebrew Beth-zatha, which has five porticoes. In these lay many invalids—blind, lame, and paralyzed—waiting for the stirring of the water; for an angel of the Lord went down at certain seasons into the pool, and stirred up the water; whoever stepped in first after the stirring of the water was made well from whatever disease that person had.

One man was there who had been ill for thirty-eight years. When Jesus saw him lying there and knew that he had been there a long time, he said to him, "Do you want to be made well?"

The sick man answered him, "Sir, I have no one to put me into the pool when the water is stirred up; and while I am making my way, someone else steps down ahead of me."

Jesus said to him, "Stand up, take your mat and walk." At once the man was made well, and he took up his mat and began to walk.

Now that day was the Sabbath. So the Jews said to the man who had been cured, "It is the Sabbath; it is not lawful for you to carry your mat." But he answered them, "The man who made me well said to me, 'Take up your mat and walk.'" They asked him, "Who is the man who said to you, 'Take it up and walk'?" Now the man who had been healed did not know who it was, for Jesus had disappeared in the crowd that was there.

Later Jesus found him in the temple and said to him, "See, you have been made well! Do not sin any more, so that nothing worse happens to you."

〜〜

"Sir, I have no one to put me into the pool when the water is stirred up; and while I am making my way, someone else steps down ahead of me."

This is a strange reply to Jesus's question, "Do you want to be made well?" The man did not actually answer Jesus's question at all. A man full of desperate passion to be healed would immediately have shouted out, "YES!!! Please, please have mercy on me and heal me!" In many incidents people did cry out to Jesus in just such a manner, but not this man. Perhaps he was not actually very eager to be healed.

The one detail given about this man's infirmity is that it had been with him for thirty-eight years. It is hard to imagine that during the course of all those years he never once managed to get himself into the healing pool. He could have convinced somebody to help him. He could have promised to, after the healing, work and pay the one who helped. Or he could have made a big fuss, explaining how long he'd been waiting and demanding that he be allowed his chance. He could have sat in the water waiting for it to move, which would have made him the first for sure. These are just a few thoughts that immediately come to mind. Imagine the possibilities one might contrive given thirty-eight years to think about it. From the words "while I am making my way" we know that this man was able to move, even if awkwardly and slowly. Yet even if he had been *completely* paralyzed, 13,879 days is still plenty of time to devise a way to get into the pool.

In many cases, when someone had been ill or possessed or crippled from birth, the Gospels reveal this fact. Since the text does not indicate that he had been crippled from birth, we can suppose that this man became crippled only later in life. This means that probably *all* of those 13,879 days occurred when he was old enough to take initiative in obtaining his healing.

Given all of this information, we can safely assume that this man was content enough not to try. He probably had grown accustomed to a life of idleness and begging. Somewhere within his heart he may have even feared the increased responsibilities that accompany increased capabilities. If he were well, he'd have no excuse to beg and so would have to work. He'd have to redefine his relationships with other people and with society. He would have to redefine himself. There are many possible reasons why this man did not have much passion to be healed.

The meaning of the name of the pool, Beth-zatha—Bethesda, as it's more commonly known—is telling. Bethesda means *House of Grace* or *Place of Outpouring*. Sometimes we find ourselves sitting around waiting for the wind of grace to pour out, stir the waters of our hearts, and change us. It likely isn't going to happen. At these times it feels like we want to change, and it appears that we believe in God's power. But in truth we don't want to change all that much. We, like the man by the pool, enjoy something about our current situation. We keep praying for God to help us, but we find that we've plateaued. Just as the man by the pool blamed his situation on the fact that nobody helped him, deep inside, we too justify our spiritual stagnation by saying, "Nobody's helping me, including God." The problem isn't that God is short on grace. The problem is that we misunderstand what grace is all about.

The Sabbath was the day of rest during which the Jews were to remember God and the fact that he created all of reality. It isn't a difficult leap to see that the essence of honoring the Sabbath is to believe that all good and all power belong to God. We remember God's omnipotence, exemplified in the fact that he is the author of all life. Here, we read that some people were upset with the man for carrying his bed on the Sabbath. Elsewhere, in fact throughout the entire New Testament, the Jews of the day misinterpreted the Sabbath rules to mean there should be no activity whatsoever on the Sabbath regardless of how useful or good. We can similarly misunderstand the idea of "saving faith." Our own faith in God's omnipotence may inhibit our initiative. Jesus was notorious for breaking the rules of the Sabbath. He frequently performed miracles on the holy day. And always, the scribes and Pharisees would become outraged.

As in many of the previous healings, the disease that is described here is manifested on many levels and in many different ways. All of these clues converge to express a single ailment: spiritual apathy based in a misunderstanding of God's omnipotence, grace, and mercy. The story of chapter 2 heals us of pathological guilt. Chapter 4 relieved us of pride- and shame-based spirituality. Guilt, pride, and shame are powerful motivations in pseudo-spirituality. Remove them, and it is easy to see how we might slip into spiritual apathy. The previous chapter showed us that that we can trust in God regardless of circumstance. This idea is summed up in the often-heard slogan *Let go and let God.*

It is easy to slightly twist this idea: *If God is doing everything, then I am not responsible for anything I do. I might as well be self-indulgent.* Or even: *If God is doing everything, why bother doing anything at all?* I have noticed a tendency within myself to alter this idea in yet another way: Because God is omnipotent, omniscient and all-loving, and since he knowingly chose to create life, life must therefore be good. Thus I need never become upset. Being upset is, in fact, a sign of spiritual immaturity. Thus my goal is to never become upset and to accept life as it is.

The adventure and joy of life is that we are free participants in its creation and healing. Divine Love heals us from within our own sense of choice, and he heals society from within our choices to love. Where would we be today if the Reverend Martin Luther King Jr. and Mahatma Ghandi had trained themselves to accept life as it is without becoming upset? Getting upset isn't the problem. The problem is that we tend to react poorly to being upset. Love dictates that we become upset by social injustice. But rather than reacting defensively, like Peter in the previous chapter, we can learn to take loving action to remedy the problem in a productive way.

Jesus, who is Love revealed in human form, became upset on occasion. He cleansed the temple of the money changers with a whip. We also read that he became upset with the hardness of the hearts of those who stood by while he healed a woman of her infirmity on the Sabbath. On several occasions he vehemently reprimanded the Pharisees, calling them a "white-washed tomb" and a "brood of vipers," among other things. I believe that Jesus's expressions of upset are all delivered for the sake of helping people move forward spiritually when nothing else is able to move the roadblock.

The saving grace of faith is sometimes believed to be a free ticket into heaven regardless of effort. In fact, it has sometimes been preached that to put effort into spiritual progress belittles one's faith in God and in saving grace. The insanity of this idea is in the failure to understand that God's grace animates us from within during our effort. If we believe we are helpless, we stop trying, and so become helpless. Our effort to evolve in love is God's grace. Faith in the Lord and making an effort to be loving are the same thing. Where there is one, the other is present. Where one does not exist, neither does the other. Faith without action is dead.

Sometimes we find ourselves seized by an apathy similar to that of this man, an apathy that is bred in false spiritual beliefs, a misunderstanding of our walk with God. Inside of us are the Pharisees commanding that we participate in no activity on the sabbath. *We dare not go to a twelve-step meeting because we need to let God heal us, not a bunch of drunks. I dare not participate in this spiritual growth group because my salvation is between me and God. We dare not look into self-help or psychology because God is the one who heals, not psychologists. I will remain calm no matter what happens, because God is in charge and I can trust him.* In all of these cases, we are failing to realize that God works through means. In the last of these cases, the means is our own self. In the former, the means are other humans who can help us move toward an improved spiritual life. We are permitted to do good on the Sabbath.

If, like the man in this miracle, we wait around for God's grace to miraculously heal us, we are putting limits on grace. We think grace only operates as an external force. We have failed to realize that grace is the essence of our efforts and heals us from within. It is true, God is responsible for our personal salvation and the salvation of our global society. But he does it only through our agency. He is the potter, and we are the clay. He is the vine, we are the branches. I believe fully both in destiny and also in human free will. God's will is that we be filled with love and so be free.

We might envision the situation in the following way. A young boy of six has a bad spinal injury, crippling his legs. The doctor says that with motion, stretching, and exercise, he may recover use of his legs. His father builds a special tandem bicycle—a seat designed for an adult in the back, and seat designed for a child in the front. The two of them go out bicycling every day. The boy loves the time with his dad, and it feels to him as if he were propelling the cycle forward at least to some degree. His father, too, encourages this sensation, telling him he's doing a great job and that he is growing stronger and healing. Soon the boy is convinced that he is providing at least 80 percent of the force moving the tandem cycle. But one day, he lets up his effort on an uphill climb and notices the cycle does not slow down. Soon the boy stops trying, and lets his legs simply be moved around by his father's motion. It doesn't take long for the father to find out. His son's posture on the bike gives him away. And from then on, when his son stops trying, his father too stops pedaling. The father knows that his son will not heal unless the boy keeps up his effort. And just as importantly, he knows that for the sake of his son's confidence, hope, and happiness, his son must feel as if he is contributing. The boy again begins to believe that he is contributing and before long that belief becomes reality. His legs recover.

I think of our relationship with God as something similar to this situation. God heals us by means of what appears to be our own effort. But the analogy is not perfect. Unlike the son in the story, when our spirit begins to heal, it is actually God's power living and working within us. God's love is our healing.

Another analogy to describe our relationship with God is found in the Old Testament. Through the mouth of Moses, the Lord commanded the children of Israel to make animal sacrifices to him. Later, through the mouths of David, Samuel, Isaiah, Micah, and others, he reminded them that he made the animals, and that what he really required was justice, mercy, and humility before God. He instructed the Israelites to sacrifice animals not because he desired them, but because he wanted the children of Israel to have a way of participating in a relationship with him and way of feeling that they could please him. And in truth, because they felt that they had pleased him with their obedience, he was indeed pleased. And the sacrifice they made was real. The meat, milk, and wool of the animals they offered could have been used by them for personal gain, but they instead offered these things to their God. The sacrifices they made were important not so much for God's sake, but for their own sakes. The same is true with us. Just as God made all the animals, so God makes all of our efforts and works. However, the effort and work we do for the sake of obeying and relating to God is important for our own sense of participating in a living relationship with a real God. We may moan to God, "Please save me!" But when we really want to be saved, we'll get up and move instead of waiting for the winds of grace to magically stir the waters of our soul.

When we begin trying to change our habits and improve our spiritual condition, it is going to take work. The work is going to be hard, and it will take a long time. It will feel exactly as if we are the ones who are wielding power. Jesus's command to the sick man was, "Take up your mat and walk." Jesus didn't touch him or pray over him. He didn't levitate him to the hospital. He just said, "Get up and move!" The same is true for us—we have to get up and take action.

Jesus's final statement to the man is, "Do not sin any more, so that nothing worse happens to you." What sin could this man possibly have committed while immobilized in a public place for years? Could it be the sin of sloth that Jesus is referring to? Are we being urged not to be spiritually apathetic?

I simultaneously believe in both destiny and free will. As a fatalist, I believe that the man was fated to thirty-eight years of being lame by the pool. Those thirty-eight years were necessary for him to be able to receive Jesus's healing. Thirty-eight years of relative idle misery are a small price to pay for an eternity of joy. As a believer in free will, I believe that the healing miracle of this story is that in Jesus, the man found the will and ability to get up and walk. The healing gave him a new destiny—to go forth and live as a healed person.

This parallels our own lives. I believe we are all destined by Divine Love to eventually be free in love. And until we are willing to consciously adopt love as our motivation and work toward making love real, we will be enslaved to selfish pursuits. Yet those years of relative misery are the necessary means that prepare us for a healing encounter with the Lord, a healing that lasts for eternity. The freedom is that we decide to get up and move of our own free will. But underlying that decision is the will of Divine Love, which is constantly putting events and people in our path to push us toward a life of love.

Another important message of this healing is that some things in our lives just take time. God invented time for a reason. I cannot judge this man for waiting thirty-eight years for a healing. It seems that thirty-eight years of waiting around was the right number to prepare. Sometimes, our willfulness has to run its course until we are either so bored or in so much pain that we finally become willing to change. Sometimes for years we struggle with genuine effort to improve some area of our life. We may see very little progress. This can lead to doubt in God. It is important to remember that this effort is not wasted. Rather than being frustrated by how far we are from the top of the mountain, we can take comfort in seeing how far we are from the bottom. Had we not been putting in effort, we likely would have plummeted into a much worse state. The goal, then, is to remain constant in our effort even as we remember that some things take time before we begin to notice improvement.

I suspect all of us are always doing the best we can with what we have—even though some people's best may look like laziness or cruelty. It is in accordance with divine will that we will eventually realize that we can add to what we have in terms of support, knowledge, and skills, and then our best will be better than before. Thus, sometimes spiritual improvement is a matter of practical strategy. Just as the man could have enlisted help from others, so we should not shy away from grabbing at anything that might improve us.

Sometimes we feel intimidated and frightened of doing or thinking anything other than what we've been fed from the pulpit. But Jesus was a free thinker, a radical, a rebel. We need to allow ourselves the freedom to think about what is true and good for ourselves. And if we see a better way than what we've been fed, we need to afford ourselves the license to pursue and live our life accordingly. God makes each of us unique, and so we will accordingly have unique views and relationships with him. The internal Pharisees will cringe at the idea of investigating other religions, philosophies, psychologies, and faiths. But Jesus is what works, and what works is Jesus. If something from Buddhism helps us to treat our children better, then the Lord of Love must be present in that technique or idea. If he weren't, we wouldn't be improved.

The self is the source of our selfishness. If we are working toward spiritual goals, we sometimes grow weary with the self. But the stone that the builders rejected has become the chief cornerstone. Our sense of self is indispensable in God's plan. Without an individual sense of self, we'd merge into oneness. No joy can pass or be shared if we don't retain some sense of distinctness from one another. Without relationship with others, there is no such thing as love. We are all united and made one in God, but within that oneness we must retain our separate selfhood. This enables us to love and appreciate other people.

To retain a sense of self, we must employ that sense of self in activity. We must keep taking the steps that propel us along the path of spiritual development. God alone draws us toward him, and all power belongs to him. But he does this by means of our legs, our hands, and our tongues.

MEDITATIONS

1. After entering into a state of meditation, imagine being this man. Imagine what it would be like to sit by a pool of water for thirty-eight years. Get in touch with the feeling of boredom and uselessness. Also get in touch with the feelings of having been slighted by life—nobody helps you. You are alone in this cruel world. Now you see Jesus come and look at you as you lie on your mat among the others. "Do you want to be made well?" he asks. You talk about how unfair it has been—nobody helps. "Stand up, take your mat and walk," he replies. You obey. What does it feel like to work your body for the first time in thirty-eight years? How do you feel in relation to your body and life? The Pharisees stop you. "You're not allowed to be carrying your mat," they say. You explain that the one who healed you commanded it. You then see Jesus again in the temple and he warns you, "Do not sin any more, so that nothing worse happens to you."

2. Meditate on what you can do to further the Lord of Love's will today.

LEAVES

1. God is in charge of all that occurs—part of what occurs is we are charged to act, as if we are autonomous and as if according to our own judgment, to further the will of Love as best we can.

2. Self is the rejected cornerstone upon which the Lord builds his church. Though sense of self is the source of all delusion and sin, it is also the needed vehicle for Love's purposes.

3. Although we trust in the Lord, we should not expect him to do

everything for us. When we see social injustice, we should take action. When we need healing ourselves, we can seek it through other people.

FRUIT

1. Meditate and or pray daily on how you can become more active in the will of the Lord.

2. Daily follow through on the messages you receive from your prayers and meditations.

3. When you get no clear answer on any given day, decide what you think would further the will of Love and do it.

4. Take a look inside to see if there is any false belief or attitude that is causing you to be spiritually apathetic.

DISCUSSION QUESTIONS

1. What was your experience of the first meditation?

2. What was your experience of your daily prayer/meditations? Did you get direct answers or not?

3. What was it like to take action each day? Did you find yourself resisting the idea?

4. Did you receive any emotional, intellectual, or attitudinal changes this week?

5. Have you seen people, like the man at the healing pool, that you believe have the opportunity to help themselves and don't? What do you think of them? If you were in Jesus's position, would you have healed that man?

6. Now think of a time in your life when you could have taken action to improve a situation and didn't. How do you think others saw you? How did you see yourself? Does thinking about this change the way you see people like the man at the healing pool?

7. Were you able to identify any false beliefs that prevent you from taking spiritual action?

11

HEALING FROM BLAME-BLINDNESS

"Neither this man nor his parents sinned; he was born blind
so that God's works might be revealed in him."

John 9:1–41

As he walked along, he saw a man blind from birth. His disciples asked him, "Rabbi, who sinned, this man or his parents, that he was born blind?" Jesus answered, "Neither this man nor his parents sinned; he was born blind so that God's works might be revealed in him. We must work the works of him who sent me while it is day; night is coming when no one can work. As long as I am in the world, I am the light of the world."

When he had said this, he spat on the ground and made mud with the saliva and spread the mud on the man's eyes, saying to him, "Go, wash in the pool of Siloam" (which means Sent). Then he went and washed and came back able to see.

The neighbors and those who had seen him before as a beggar began to ask, "Is this not the man who used to sit and beg?" Some were saying, "It is he." Others were saying, "No, but it is someone like him." He kept saying, "I am the man." But they kept asking him, "Then how were your eyes opened?" He answered, "The man called Jesus made mud, spread it on my eyes, and said to me, 'Go to Siloam and wash.' Then I went and washed and received my sight." They said to him, "Where is he?" He said, "I do not know."

They brought to the Pharisees the man who had formerly been blind. Now it was a sabbath day when Jesus made the mud and opened his eyes. Then the Pharisees also began to ask him how he had received his sight. He said to them, "He put mud on my eyes. Then I washed, and now I see." Some of the Pharisees said, "This man is not from God, for he does not observe the sabbath." But others said, "How can a man who is a sinner perform such signs?" And they were divided.

So they said again to the blind man, "What do you say about him? It was your eyes he opened." He said, "He is a prophet." The Jews did not believe that he had been blind and had received his sight until they called the parents of the man who had received his sight and asked them, "Is this your son, who you say was born blind? How then does he now see?" His parents answered, "We know that this is our son, and that he was born blind; but we do not know how it is that now he sees, nor do we know who opened his eyes. Ask him, he is of age. He will speak for himself." His parents said this because they were afraid of the Jews; for the Jews had already agreed that anyone who confessed Jesus to be the Messiah would be put out of the synagogue. Therefore his parents said, "He is of age; ask him."

So for the second time they called the man who had been born blind, and they said to him, "Give glory to God! We know that this man is a sinner." He answered, "I do not know whether he is a sinner. One thing I do know, that though I was blind, now I see." They said to him, "What did he do to you? How did he open your eyes?" He answered them, "I have told you already, and you would not listen. Why do you want to hear it again? Do you also want to become his disciples?"

Then they reviled him, saying, "You are his disciple, but we are disciples of Moses. We know that God has spoken to Moses, but as for this man, we do not know where he comes from." The man answered, "Here is an astonishing thing! You do not know where he comes from, and yet he opened my eyes. We know that God does not listen to sinners, but he does listen to one who worships him and obeys his will. Never since the world began has it been heard that anyone opened the eyes of a person born blind. If this man were not from God, he could do nothing." They answered him, "You were born entirely in sins, and are you trying to teach us?" And they drove him out.

Jesus heard that they had driven him out, and when he found him, he said, "Do you believe in the Son of Man?" He answered, "And who is he, sir? Tell me, so that I may believe in him." Jesus said to him, "You have seen him, and the one speaking with you is he." He said, "Lord, I believe." And he worshiped him. Jesus said, "I came into this world for judgment so that those who do not see may see, and those who do see may become blind."

Some of the Pharisees near him heard this and said to him, "Surely we are not blind, are we?" Jesus said to them, "If you were blind, you would not have sin. But now that you say, 'We see,' your sin remains."

Although investigating each and every miracle reviewed in this book has proved a profound and healing experience for me, the impact of this miracle has been perhaps the most dramatic and liberating of them all.

Let's start at the beginning, with the disciples' question, "Teacher, who sinned, this man or his parents that he was born blind?" From the time I was a small child, I was well aware that people around me were suffering. And as I grew, I came to see that suffering is a widespread, almost universal human experience. Like the disciples, I wanted to know why. Why do people suffer? When I arrived in high school and college, I came to see that I was by no means alone in my wonder. Countless pages and classroom hours have been devoted to the problem of evil.

But the disciples didn't simply ask, "Why is the man blind?" They wanted to know on whom to lay the blame. And it is my experience that when confronted by suffering, our human tendency is to likewise seek someone or something to blame. Sometimes we blame God. "If God actually cared about us, he'd not allow those children to starve."

Some people blame Adam and Eve. Although a commonly accepted idea, it seems slightly off to blame all the suffering of humanity on the ingestion of a fruit. I prefer to read those first few chapters of Genesis as an allegorical description of the early stages of every individual's spiritual journey. Adam and Eve represent aspects of our being that, once innocent, eventually choose to seek freedom outside of God's plan.

In some cases we blame upbringing. "He grew up in a broken home in a rough neighborhood." More and more we blame genetics, believing people are programmed to harm others by their genes. Finally, we often blame individuals. "If my spouse didn't spend so much time working, I could go out and have fun more often." "If my parents hadn't been so overprotective, I'd be able to do more for myself." All of these are attempts to solve the problem of evil.

In short, the problem of evil is this: *If God truly is omnipotent, omniscient, and all-loving, why is there evil and suffering?* All those classroom hours, all those articles and tomes, all the pondering devoted to this question find their true resolution in Jesus's singular and beautiful sentence, "Neither this man nor his parents sinned; he was born blind so that God's works might be revealed in him." In one simple sentence, Jesus cuts through the blame game altogether. In this sentence Jesus solves the age-old dilemma, the problem of evil. In effect, the Lord of Love is telling us that to look for the source and cause of suffering is to be asking the wrong question. Suffering does not exist for the sake of judging and blaming; it exists so that God's glory can be revealed.

Here, Jesus was only addressing the issue of the blind man, and not the entire issue of suffering. Elsewhere, more than once, Jesus entreats us not to judge or blame. Rather, when confronted with suffering, we are to pray for the perpetrators. In one lesson, Jesus tells us to first remove the log from our own eye before we judge our neighbor. Jesus is equating a judgmental outlook with the log that induces blindness. If we want to see reality as it truly is, we must remove the log of judgment from our eye altogether. The questions,

"Who sinned?" and "Who is to blame for suffering?" arise from a desire to pass judgment. When we find ourselves asking these questions, we can know that we are in a state of spiritual blindness.

In the miracle we are now examining, it first appears that the main event is Jesus healing a man of physical blindness. But as has been the case in each and every miracle we've looked at, the healing goes much deeper and broader than first meets the eye. Jesus is here offering to heal us of spiritual blindness, a blindness that most of us don't even realize we suffer.

The Pharisees, here again, are sure that they know the truth. They are sure that they are in the right. They judge Jesus as a troublemaker, a heretic, and a liar. Their judgment blinds them to the very obvious truth that Jesus has worked an astounding, unheard-of miracle—a man born blind has been given vision. The Pharisees personify that part of us that wants to believe that we can separate the good from the bad and that we are justified in judging between them.

Judging creates a false sense of power and position. We imagine we see the situation clearly and so can pass judgment. This power and position offers us a false sense of safety that caters to that deepest form of selfish fear—self-preservation and self-promotion. We are getting to the heart of darkness, and Jesus offers a blazing beam of light to dispel the shadows. We love power because power makes us feel safe and invincible. The desire for power is actually indicative of deep-seated insecurity and fear.

Fear and insecurity are the heart of selfishness. If we can overcome these, we are liberated indeed. And it is this liberation that Jesus is offering us here in this lesson. It is a freedom to love without any strings. It is a freedom to enjoy life without any fears. It is liberation from the prison of self into the spacious meadows of love and grace.

We only have two fundamental options on how to view the problem of evil; either there is someone to blame or there isn't. In this story the Pharisees are almost obsessed with pointing the finger, whereas Jesus clearly says that no one is to blame. Suffering is not a punishment, or even a call to judge the perpetrator, but a means to an end—the glorification of God.

What of other cases of suffering—poverty, war, violence, abuse, abandonment, loss, and the like? In many cases, placing blame seems like an obvious choice. The perpetrating dictator of war appears to deserve blame. We instinctively feel that the abusive man is to blame for the suffering he inflicts on his victim. And while these and all people most definitely must be held accountable for their deeds, the deeper look of love reveals that these people too are links in a chain of suffering.

Before we judge another as the source or cause of evil and suffering, we should ask, "Why did this man or woman commit this act of violence?" If we are truthful, we'll find that we can't answer this question. In fact, if we are honest, we don't know why anyone is who they are or why they do what they do. Why does one woman become a loving mother but her sister an abusive, alcoholic mother? Why does one man have the quality of sympathy but another have none? Is it upbringing? Is it choice? Is it genetics? Is it God's will? Of course, we cannot discern the answer. But we can know for sure that those who do harm to others are not at peace and do not know true joy—the joy of love. They are victims of mental and emotional slavery. The perpetrator is a victim on a spiritual level.

Every time we look at another human with even a shred of disdain or contempt, we have passed a false judgment. We have assumed we know why they did this or that misdeed—*freely chosen malice*. Our fearful selfishness has falsely assumed the seat of judgment, a seat that belongs to none other than God himself. We have no ability or right to sit in that seat. We cannot afford even the slightest judgmental attitude if we want to be right with God, or if we want to see life as it truly is.

And if we refuse to sit in that seat of judgment, we awaken to the fact that God's only judgment is one of pure mercy, love, and forgiveness. We suddenly see life in a whole new way—we see that it is full of wonder. We come to realize that we were blind. Through these new eyes of nonjudgment we see that life is utterly beautiful because it is overflowing with inexpressible love and mercy. We will rejoice and praise God as loudly and as purely as did this blind man; for we, too, will awaken to the fact that we were born blind, but now we see.

The story of the blind man's healing illustrates the polar dichotomy of what our minds are like when we hold on to judgment, and what our minds can be when we allow ourselves to surrender power and release all judgments completely. We see that not only do the Pharisees judge Jesus, but they try to incite the man and his parents to judge him as well. In contrast, we see how the blind man refuses to judge Jesus. He simply says, "I do not know whether he is a sinner. One thing I do know, that though I was blind, now I see." He's just stating the facts with no judgment for good or ill.

At this point in the story, the Pharisees begin to judge the healed man as well. They "revile" him, cast him out, and pronounce him born "entirely in sins." And in the end, Jesus explains the heart of the message: "I came into this world for judgment so that those who do not see may see, and those who do see may become blind." Jesus is saying that when we presume to see clearly enough to judge others, self, life, or God, we are in fact blind with the log in our eye. But when we admit that we are too blind to judge another, than we are beginning to see clearly. The story continues: "Some of the Pharisees near him heard this and said to him, 'Surely we are not blind, are we?' Jesus said to them, 'If you were blind, you would not have sin. But now that you say, "We see," your sin remains.'"

This seemingly simple response by Jesus opens up into a whole new and profound concept. Not only does judgment blind us, it is the source of sin. If this is true, the imperative to withhold all judgment is of paramount importance in our spiritual walk. Let's take a look at the radical idea that all sin stems back to judgment.

In the Garden of Eden, it was the eating of the fruit of the Tree of Knowledge of Good and Evil that began the cycle of sin. In other words, it was the desire to know and so judge between good and evil that led to all sin. We have already noted that when we judge others we have greatly overestimated our own abilities in that we have assumed the throne of God. God is the only one with enough wisdom and love to make accurate and good judgments. To make ourselves out to be God is as grave and deep a sin as any. It is the "original sin." And yet most of us do it all the time. We judge the day as "bad." We judge the weather as "horrible." But in judging the day and the weather, we judge the Author of these things. Who are we to judge any aspect of reality as bad when it is God's reality? And, of course, we are so easily caught up in judging others to be less than ourselves; to be worthy of our actual or contemplated revenge, disdain, and hostility.

What if we, like the healed blind man, refused to judge? What had been a "bad day with horrible weather" is now a day in which we witness God quenching the thirst of the plants and washing the dirt off of the houses. So as soon as we refuse to judge, things immediately look better. There are no more "bad days" but simply learning experiences. And now that we are no longer carrying around hostility and judgments against other people, we notice that peace and serenity fill in the empty mental space. We may even find some joy and genuine love creeping in. Where once we felt hate, we feel compassion—even for those who create much pain. We see them now as people who are hurting and blind.

Without all the anger inside, we'll find we no longer feel that desperate need to tranquilize ourselves with drink, drugs, sex, gambling, success, or other pleasures of the selfhood. So maybe it is actually true that all sin arises from judgment. Emanuel Swedenborg put it this way:

Everything good and true comes from the Lord and everything evil and false from hell. If people believed in this, the true situation, they could not be held accountable for any failing or have evil imputed to them. People believe that it all comes from themselves, though, so they adopt evil as their own. This is what their belief does. The evil therefore clings to them and cannot be detached. (*Secrets of Heaven* §6324)

If nothing originates in the human heart, how can we judge anyone?

But of course the practice is difficult. It's hard to say, "Ah, what a wonderful day—a blessing from God!" if, for example, we are hit and seriously injured by a drunk driver. No, it's not easy, but it is the way. It is the way prescribed by Jesus, and it is the only way by which we can arrive at our ultimate destination of peace and goodwill toward all people. When we are slighted by others, the best thing we can do—as Jesus teaches—is to pray for the other's well-being. As Jesus says, if we love our own friends, what is that? The goal is to learn how to love our enemies. The only way we can do that is to stop blaming.

There is a part within all of us that reacts adversely to the effort of refusing to judge. That inner voice wants the satisfaction of pointing a finger and laying blame squarely "where it belongs!" Plus, it rubs us the wrong way to think that evil reveals God. We wonder how it is that evil—murder, rape, slavery, torture, etc.—can possibly be for the glory of God.

Evil in all its manifestations is an opportunity for the revelation of God's glory—not in and of itself, but in our response to that evil. When we learn to really love people as children of God despite their evils and sins, we allow God's glory to shine out powerfully and visibly. Has anyone ever shown you love even after you hurt them? Such an event often alters who we are. To receive this kind of love inspires us leave off from our own sins. Sometimes our lives are so degraded by sin and evil that we can't believe in our own worth. Without believing in our value, we have little motivation and little chance of changing our ways. But when someone reaches out to us with earnest love, that love can catalyze a change in our lifestyle. That love is of course God's healing love. So we see that the suffering was "that God's works might be revealed."

When the blind man gained his sight, God's power and glory were indeed revealed. When we are able to continue loving others even in the face of their sins, God's love will likewise be revealed.

Not only is the perpetrator one step closer to healing, but the one who loved has also grown one step closer to God. He has reached out and visited the brother who was spiritually sick and imprisoned, and so he has done it to God too.

Jesus wonderfully exemplifies this point in the parable of the prodigal son. The sin and waste of the younger son's life were transformed into amazing joy and beauty by means of the love of the father. That younger son came to know the endless mercy and love of the father in a way that he likely wouldn't have otherwise realized. Of course, this doesn't mean that we should experiment with sin. But it does show how God's glory is revealed even within evil. Sin is the manure from which the flower of love grows.

A baby interprets a shot in the arm as bad, not yet able to see the ultimate good. When we experience persecution or misfortune, it feels bad. But if we refuse to feel judgmental against God, against others, and against ourselves, we'll soon see the bigger picture. We'll see how even these events that seem negative are ultimately part of God's plan for good. In the far past, during times of mass extinction, 60 to 90 percent of all species of life on earth have several times been simultaneously, completely annihilated. It doesn't get much worse than that. And yet, after each mass extinction, life has flourished in an explosion of new, more diverse, complex, and wondrous species. Just as Jesus ultimately couldn't be killed, so God's love and life can't be snuffed out. It always triumphs in the end, because it is the basis on which all of reality exists.

I find it absolutely vital to believe in an afterlife. When things are overwhelming and seem hopeless, it helps so much to get the grand perspective that Jesus offers us. He tells us that he has "prepared a place" for us; that there are "many mansions" in his Father's home. He says that if he is lifted up, which he was, he will draw *all* people to himself. We have the promise at the end of the Bible of the golden city, New Jerusalem, where there is no more pain, war, suffering, or tears, and where nothing corrupt can enter. We may wonder for whom that happy afterlife awaits. If we have accepted the message of this healing, we are no longer concerned with who enters heaven and who does not. We know that we know nothing about it. We know that God is just and loving and that he will sort it out properly. We also know that it is our job to assume the best, not only about others but also about God.

I've mentioned before that I have had trouble believing things. Believing in a happy afterlife has been no different. What helps me believe are the practical, here-and-now benefits of that belief. When I believe that earthly life is not the final end but only a training ground or place of preparation, it makes the suffering here more tolerable. I am liberated to stop judging it as unbearable. It's like night and day. If night were all there were, it would be quite unhappy. But night is only temporary and lends contrast to day. Winter gives way to spring and actually accentuates and amplifies the beauty and joy of spring. So because belief in a happy eternity after death makes me a better person, I'm willing to believe.

When we let go of the good vs. evil judgment we will begin to see love and goodness in situations that otherwise seemed bleak and hopeless. What we used to write off as bad we now see as opportunities for growth and development. When a driver cuts us off, we see it as a chance to surrender our temper and so grow closer to God. We take the opportunity to pray for the other driver. We begin to live in this way all the time: every moment and every event is an opportunity to choose God's way and God's love. It takes a lifetime of practice, but just like any other spiritual muscle, the more we employ it, the stronger it grows. We may feel depressed about the state of the world. Indeed, it does often seem hopeless. But for me to judge the human race as hopeless doesn't help anyone else, and certainly not myself. Instead, I can see chances to love and help others. We can see opportunities for God to work his miracles. We can truly say, "Thank you Lord, for this blessing that I do not yet understand."

This brings me to an important point, though it may seem like a tangent. With modern communication as it is, we are constantly exposed to the horrors that occur around the world. Most of the time, we are without recourse for action to help. In Isaiah we read the following words: "Those . . . who stop their ears from hearing of bloodshed and shut their eyes from looking on evil, they will live on the heights; their refuge will be the fortresses of rocks; their food will be supplied, their water assured" (Isa. 33:15–16). To be exposed to all the major catastrophes and wars of the world each and every day greatly skews our vision of reality. If we take a look at each day, each moment, as it is here and now, most of the time things are not that bad. And when there is some injustice or suffering in our immediate surroundings, we are much better equipped and able to help alleviate the situation. Perhaps we should only watch or read the news when we have determined ahead of time that we are going to help solve some one issue that we will be exposed to. We will make a donation; or we will adopt a suffering child; or we will write to our congressperson. What good is bathing in the atrocities of the day when we aren't going to do anything about them? It is much easier to stop judging life as hopeless or miserable when we aren't constantly exposed to the worst problems on our earth. Here and now is a lot easier to deal with. Or, if we are going to watch and read the news, we should at least maintain an attitude of hope in the light of God's loving guidance.

Let's take a closer look at the actual method Jesus used to heal the man of his blindness. He spat on the ground, made clay, anointed the eyes of the blind man and sent him to wash in the pool named Siloam, which means "Sent." In these details we see the way that Jesus heals us of a judging and blind spirit.

The clay that Jesus made was no ordinary clay. The dirt he used, it is true, was nothing special. However, this earth was mixed with the saliva of God. When we look out into reality with our eyes, there is plenty enough trouble to make us worry, and we judge it as a scary place to live. The reality of life on earth with all of its troubles is represented by the dirt. Our blindness arises when we look at earthly reality without mixing it with spiritual doctrine. The spit from Jesus's mouth mixed into the dirt was what made the clay a healing salve. So it is with us: when we allow the Word of God—which, like spit, emanates from his mouth—to temper our earthly outlook, things begin to look very different indeed. All of natural creation exists as a training ground for an eternity of joy and peace with God and with one another. This is the truth. All of the pain and problems of earthly life are opportunities for our spiritual development and will ultimately be bent to our eternal good. This is the spiritual saliva of God that tempers the dirt of earthly life into a healing salve.

After applying the salve, Jesus told the man to wash in Siloam or "Sent." It helps me to relax, trust God, and stop judging when I remember that we didn't choose to be born. We have all been elected by God into being here on earth. We have been "sent" to earth. The word "sent" implies a mission, a purpose. When there is a purpose to be accomplished, hard work, setbacks, and troubles are invariably a part of what we face. Life on earth isn't supposed to be easy. If it were easy, we'd never have the chance to develop our spiritual strengths: perseverance, love in adversity, serenity amidst turmoil, faith in the face of strife. This is the training ground, and we've been "sent" here by God to accomplish our spiritual training.

Once we are seeing life through the nonjudgmental lens of love, we also come to realize why evil and sin must be permitted: if we are going to be evolved into loving individuals, we must first be given the freedom to not love, to be selfish. Only then can we experience a life of love as something we choose and want for ourselves.

In summary, God's glory is revealed by means of evil in at least six ways.

1. We need at least some trouble to be able to appreciate the joy and peace of love.
2. When we are confronted by problems and evil, it is an opportunity for us to grow spiritually by facing those problems with love.
3. When we show love to others despite their sins, we are letting God's love and glory shine out onto this earth.

4. When that love shines out, it affects the people receiving the love and catalyzes change in their lives. They can start moving away from sin and toward God. This is true when others show us love as well.

5. When we begin practicing this kind of love in our everyday lives, we begin to see God's love and glory shining out in all circumstances. Our eyes open to the fact that all moments are gifts from God, even the challenging ones. All moments are opportunities for the growth of love.

6. For us to grow into love from freedom, we must be given the opportunity to sin.

Next time we feel judgmental of others, self, God, or life itself, let's stop and remember this healing. We can temper our view of reality with the truth that emanates from God's mouth: life is "very good," and trouble leads to our eternal blessing. He has "overcome the world," and so we can be of good cheer. We have been sent here to grow and learn. Every problem we face is a blessing in disguise. An eternity of happiness awaits us after the veil of this life is lifted.

As long as we judge, we are blind to the reality of heaven all around us; instead we see hell. Delusion is hell and hell is delusion. We enter into perception of God's love as soon as we become willing to stop judging—period. The Kingdom of Heaven is all around us and within us, waiting for us notice it.

So what is the new vision we have gained? What is it that we now see that causes us to say of our past, "I was blind!" We now see that all events are the means by which God's love is ever more deeply revealed to the human race. In short, everything is ultimately the continuously opening revelation of God's pure love. We might summarize the healing message of this story in these startling words: *Everything is in and of God, and so everything is ultimately good. Hell is simply an inability to see reality as it is. Life is the ever-unfolding manifestation of Divine Love.*

God's love is reality itself. And the ups and downs that occur in our lives are manifestations of the progressive leading and revealing of that love. Before, in our blindness, we saw despair and fear and evil. Now we see nothing but the process of God gaining victory over our blind delusions.

MEDITATIONS

1. After entering into a state of meditation, imagine yourself as the blind man. Imagine having never seen. Imagine how much you'd love to see. You are sure that you are a sinner for having been born blind. You hear the disciples of Jesus asking who is the sinner, you or your parents. And you hear Jesus's response: "Neither this man nor his parents sinned; he was born blind so that God's works might be revealed in him." Let those words sink in—you and your problems exist so that God's glory might be revealed. You hear Jesus pick up some dirt and spit into it. You then feel him rub it onto your eyes and tell you to go wash in the pool of Sent. You grope your way to the pool and begin to splash the cool water onto your face. It feels wonderful. You cautiously, hopefully open your eyes. You feel ecstatic as you begin to see the reflection of the sun on the undulating water. You are seeing the world for the first time! Let yourself dwell on the feelings of joy. You stand up and start proclaiming to all you meet, "I can see!" The Pharisees begin to pester you and your parents, but you couldn't care less. You are full of the joy of vision! You go back to Jesus and he says, "Do you believe in the Son of Man?" You reply "Who is he, sir? Tell me, so that I may believe in him." Jesus responds, "You have seen him, and the one speaking with you is he." You say, "Lord, I believe!" and you worship him.

2. Meditate on reality—the birds, the rocks, the people in your life, the events of history, and your past—from an attitude of nonjudgment. See them with gratitude as aspects of God's divine plan of unfolding love.

3. Meditate on any of the ideas listed under "Leaves" that calls out to you.

LEAVES

1. We are blind and cannot properly judge any event or person.
2. All sin arises from judgment.
3. All problems exist so that God's power and love might be revealed.
4. God is in charge of everything and he is all-powerful, all-loving and all-wise.
5. There is a wonderful afterlife awaiting us.
6. Reality is the ever-opening flower of God's love.
7. We've been sent here to grow and learn.

FRUIT

1. Spend this week refusing to judge anything at all. Try to notice judgmental feelings and ideas. When they arise, replace them with an admission of blindness. Replace the judgment with love by engaging in the rest of the fruits below.

2. Whenever we find ourselves with negative feelings toward people and events, we pray for the blessing and healing of the person against whom we feel judgment. We may use the faith prayer, "Lord, I believe; help my disbelief!"

3. Thank and praise the Lord of Love every day.

4. Look for the good in all people and events.

5. Work to improve situations that are upsetting.

6. If we find ourselves weighed down by the events we see or hear in the media, we can stop watching and reading the news except when we are prepared to make a change in relation to what we see.

DISCUSSION QUESTIONS

1. Has anything remarkable happened to you this week? Did the Lord touch you this week in a special way concerning or not concerning the message of this miracle?

2. What was your experience of the meditations?

3. What was your experience of the exercises?

4. What was it like to spend a week refusing to judge anything at all?

5. Share an example of a time when someone wronged you. Is it hard to refuse to judge the person? What did you feel when you tried?

6. When you heard those stories, did you judge the people who committed the wrong? Or perhaps the person who was sharing the experience? Take a moment to reflect on your reaction. How did you feel as you made the judgment? How does it feel when you try to let go?

7. If any value was gained from this miracle, how can we incorporate it and sustain it in our daily lives?

12

RESURRECTION FROM SPIRITUAL DEATH

"I am the resurrection and the life."

John 11:1–44

Now a certain man was ill, Lazarus of Bethany, the village of Mary and her sister Martha. Mary was the one who anointed the Lord with perfume and wiped his feet with her hair; her brother Lazarus was ill. So the sisters sent a message to Jesus, "Lord, he whom you love is ill." But when Jesus heard it, he said, "This illness does not lead to death; rather it is for God's glory, so that the Son of God may be glorified through it." Accordingly, though Jesus loved Martha and her sister and Lazarus, after having heard that Lazarus was ill, he stayed two days longer in the place that he was.

Then after this he said to the disciples, "Let us go to Judea again." The disciples said to him, "Rabbi, the Jews were just now trying to stone you, and are you going there again?" Jesus answered, "Are there not twelve hours of daylight? Those who walk during the day do not stumble, because they see the light of this world. But those who walk at night stumble, because the light is not in them." After saying this, he told them, "Our friend Lazarus has fallen asleep, but I am going there to awaken him." The disciples said to him, "Lord, if he has fallen asleep, he will be all right." Jesus, however, had been speaking about his death, but they thought that he was referring merely to sleep. Then Jesus told them plainly, "Lazarus is dead. For your sake I am glad I was not there, so that you may believe. But let us go to him." Thomas, who was called the Twin, said to his fellow disciples, "Let us also go, that we may die with him."

When Jesus arrived, he found that Lazarus had already been in the tomb four days. Now Bethany was near Jerusalem, some two miles away, and many of the Jews had come to Martha and Mary to console them about their brother. When Martha heard that Jesus was coming, she went and met him, while Mary stayed at home. Martha said to Jesus, "Lord, if you had been here, my brother would not have died. But even now I know that God will give you whatever you ask of him." Jesus said to her, "Your brother will rise again." Martha said to him, "I know that he will rise again in the resurrection on the last day." Jesus said to her, "I am the resurrection and the life. Those who believe in me, even though they die, will live, and everyone who lives and believes in me will never die. Do you believe this?" She said to him, "Yes, Lord, I believe that you are the Messiah, the Son of God, the one coming into the world."

When she had said this, she went back and called her sister Mary, and told her privately, "The Teacher is here and is calling for you." And when she heard this, she got up quickly and went to him. Now Jesus had not yet come to the village, but was still at the place where Martha had met him. The Jews who were with her in the house, consoling her, saw Mary get up quickly and go out. They followed her because they thought that she was going to the tomb to weep there.

When Mary came where Jesus was and saw him, she knelt at his feet and said to him, "Lord, if you had been there, my brother would not have died." When Jesus saw her weeping, and the Jews who came with her also weeping, he was greatly disturbed in the spirit and deeply moved. He said, "Where have you laid him?" They said to him, "Lord, come and see."

Jesus wept. So the Jews said, "See how he loved him!" But some of them said, "Could not he who opened the eyes of the blind man have kept this man from dying?"

Then Jesus, again greatly disturbed, came to the tomb. It was a cave, and a stone was lying against it. Jesus said, "Take away the stone." Martha, the sister of the dead man, said to him, "Lord, already there is a stench because he has been dead four days." Jesus said to her, "Did I not tell you that if you believed, you would see the glory of God?" So they took away the stone. And Jesus looked upward and said, "Father, I thank you for having heard me. I knew that you always hear me, but I have said this for the sake of the crowd standing here, so that they may believe that you sent me." When he had said this, he cried out with a loud voice, "Lazarus, come out!" The dead man came out, his hands and feet bound with strips of cloth, and his face wrapped in a cloth. Jesus said to them, "Unbind him, and let him go."

<hr />

"Out of the eater came something to eat. Out of the strong came something sweet."

Samson spoke these words as a riddle to confound the Philistines after he killed a lion and later found a beehive with honey within the carcass (Judges 14:14). In the events of Samson, we can see foreshadowing of Jesus's life. Samson loved a treacherous woman and lost his life due to his love for her. So Jesus lost his life for his love for the human race and our treachery. Samson was willing to die for the sake of conquering the Philistines and delivering Israel from their oppression. Jesus was willing to die for the sake of conquering death and hell and saving the human race from their oppression. We can also see the masterwork of Jesus within this riddle.

Samson's enemies answered his riddle with these words, "What is stronger than a lion? And what is sweeter than honey?" But I might answer the riddle this way, "What is stronger than death? And what is sweeter than the salvation of Jesus—a soul at peace and full of goodwill?"

In this chapter we will see how Jesus amazingly brings his peace, love, joy, and salvation into our lives not by our strengths, but by the fact of our spiritual death. It is our total lack of spiritual power and fortitude that allows us to receive the Lord's wonderful gift of a soul at rest and a spirit full of goodwill. Out of the strong, comes something sweet; out of the eater, something to eat.

In the previous chapter we saw that the only true interpretation of reality is that it is the perfect manifestation of God's pure and infinite love for us. It is nothing but mercy and grace. Jesus told us that he is the true light of the world. Only when we see life in and from that light do we see correctly. In that light we see that all evil and suffering are steps on the way, opportunities for the glory of God to be revealed. And then we see that all of our suffering and even our evil arises only within our own delusional sense of reality.

Jesus reiterates this idea in this chapter as well: "Are there not twelve hours of daylight? Those who walk during the day do not stumble, because they see the light of this world. But those who walk at night stumble, because the light is not in them." Again, Jesus is telling us that he is the light of the world. In order to survive, it is imperative that we learn to walk in him, with him. In trusting him completely, despite appearances, we begin to see life for what it actually is—the self-revealing manifestation of pure Divine Love. "I am the resurrection and the life," Jesus says to Mary. "Those who believe in me, even though they die, will live, and everyone who lives and believes in me will never die. Do you believe this?" Are we able to believe in Jesus as he is asking us to believe—that because of his life, all of life on earth is somehow redeemed; that his love for us causes even the most heinous agony of life on earth to bow down and serve the purpose of eternal well-being?

Many of us, much of the time, fall short of this ideal. We often see life as a great deal less than God's pure love and mercy. Life frequently seems to be a difficult string of trials. It sometimes seems downright malicious. But at the same time, in our better states, we are able to see and feel God's divine love with us, permeating all of reality.

Sometimes our state of mind can change quite suddenly. We may wake up in the morning feeling grouchy and resentful, but having met an old friend, we feel grateful and happy by evening. Such changes in mood and mindset are so common that we don't think twice about them. But careful analysis reveals something very odd. In the morning, we believed life to be a chore, maybe even worthless. But by evening, our heart says that life is wonderful. In the span of just twelve hours, our view of reality has made a 180-degree turnaround. Which perception of reality is true? Our heart is constantly fluctuating through different states throughout our lives. At any given moment, we think, "Yes, this is me. This is what I feel. This is what I think. And this is what I believe." But from moment to moment our thoughts, our desires, and even our core beliefs change.

An alcoholic wakes up with an unspeakable headache and proclaims, "I hate alcohol! I will never drink again!" But by evening he is again reaching for his "only true friend." We saw in chapter three that the negative desires within us are best seen as a foreign force within our spirit, a hoard of devils. Only by separating our sense of self from the addictive desires do we have hope of finding liberation from their dictates.

Similarly, we saw in chapters 7, 8, and 9 that none of our faith, our good motives, or works are "ours." Rather, we are like a foreigner, a guest in God's land. We receive these things, but they are not ours. They are God's and God's alone. Drawing the two ideas together, we can see that we are neither the negative powers within our minds, nor the positive. We are, as the prophets said, empty vessels. We are but pots of clay. In Buddhist tradition one of the ultimate truths to realize and sense is our inherent emptiness. In twelve-step culture the foundational truth underlying all sobriety is expressed in step one: *We admitted that we were powerless—that our lives had become unmanageable.* The greatest spiritual minds of every tradition all arrive at the same truth: human beings are in essence empty vessels. Jesus, much more than a great human thinker, phrased it this way: "I am the vine, you are the branches. Those who abide in me and I in them bear much fruit, because apart from me you can do nothing" (John 15:5).

The fact of our emptiness is a truth vital to our birth into spiritual life. In and of ourselves, we are nothing and can do nothing. The body is a vehicle and servant that executes the dictates of thought. We would never think of an automobile as our essential selfhood. Our body is also not our essential selfhood. Thought in turn is the vehicle and servant of the dictates of will. Therefore thought is also not our essential selfhood. As chapter 3 explained, non-loving desires are created by external forces that possess us. And as we saw in several of the previous chapters, loving motivations all arise from the one true love, who is God. All Love is one and Love is divine. Thus we are neither our evil desires nor are we our desire to realize love. Self cannot be defined by body, by thoughts, or by the desires of our will.

If we are not our body, not our thoughts, and not the motivations of our will, then what can we say is our true self? The only thing left is consciousness itself. Yet pure consciousness has no characteristics and is identical in all of us. So if we were to say that this pure consciousness is the fundamental self, we would have to say that the self is the same for all of us, which isn't really a "self" at all. We'd also have to admit that this pure consciousness is not created by us, but is given to us to experience. In other words, it is God's. So in the final analysis, we must admit that we are without any actual self. We are truly empty. This is our spiritual poverty.

The emptiness of self causes life after death to be a riddle: who or what, exactly, is saved or condemned?

There is not just one story about a man named Lazarus who dies and is resurrected, but two. And I don't think it is a coincidence that the same name is used in relation to the same subject, life after death. In Luke, Jesus tells us about the impoverished Lazarus who begs for scraps and crumbs of bread at the gate of a miserly rich man who gives him none. The dogs come and lick poor Lazarus's sores as he dies. The angels carry him up to the bosom of Abraham.

The wealthy man also dies, and he finds himself in the fiery torments of hell. He begs for Lazarus to cool his burning tongue with a few drops of water. But because of a great gulf or emptiness between the two, Lazarus cannot oblige. Then the rich man begs that his five brothers be warned of their fiery fate. But again he is told that if the brothers would not believe Moses and the prophets they would not be persuaded "even if someone rises from the dead" (Luke 16:31).

On first appearance, this parable seems to say that people who are self-indulgent and mean-spirited go to hell, while those who suffer on earth go to heaven. But this literal interpretation doesn't make much sense. Is being materially poor really the prerequisite for heaven? Jesus opened the Sermon on the Mount with the words, "Blessed are the poor *in spirit*, for theirs is the kingdom of heaven" (Matt. 5:3). From this we can assume that the poverty of Lazarus refers to spiritual and not earthly poverty. And the truth is that we are all spiritually impoverished. None of us have an iota of personal spiritual strength.

All of us have passed through greedy, selfish states similar to that of the miserly rich man, and all of us have also experienced mournful states in which we are acutely aware of our spiritual poverty. Both characters in Jesus's parable reflect states that we experience within our spirit. Sometimes the greedy, selfish force within us dominates over the Lazarus within us. The name Lazarus is derived from the Hebrew name El'azar, which means *Helper*. The part of us that is completely destitute of any spiritual wealth or power at all is a "helper" to God's plan. It is because of our spiritual death that Jesus can resurrect us to spiritual life, his life.

In the parable, after death, the tables are turned. A sense of self-importance is banished to Hades, but acknowledgment of utter spiritual destitution is raised up into God's peace and joy in heaven. Our selfish desires cannot be anything but miserable and self-serving. The unavoidable abode of selfishness is within the fires of its own hell. God's selfless love and joy simply can't communicate or be received by selfishness. It is as impossible as trying to give sunlight to night without changing into day. Or it is like trying to give heat to cold without altering its fundamental coldness. On the other hand, awareness of our spiritual poverty is able to receive and be animated by Divine Love.

The basis from which all the non-loving desires emerge is the underlying delusion that we have power and an autonomous self-hood. Like the rich man in the parable, we feast on the idea that we are spiritually rich. We have stolen from God and mistaken God's riches for our own. Once our sense of self is inflated, we fall prey to the selfish desires that arise from faith in a sense of self. We have made ourselves vulnerable to the Legions discussed in chapter 3.

This is why it is necessary for us to come to see our inherent spiritual death before we can be resurrected into the eternal life of Divine Love. This is why Jesus says, "Lazarus is dead. For your sake I am glad I was not there, so that you may believe." Jesus was glad that Lazarus died so that his glory, the life-giving power of Divine Love, might be revealed.

In this story, when Jesus said that he intended to go to Judea, where men had plotted to kill him, Thomas says, "Let us also go, that we might die with him." Thomas's love for Jesus propelled him to be willing to face death alongside him. In this we are given to understand how we can come to accept the fact that we are spiritually dead, the prerequisite for spiritual life. Like Thomas, our love for the Lord Jesus Christ is the path. We can actively work to increase our love for Jesus. We can study his life and words. Like Thomas, we can challenge him to appear to us personally and not simply accept his authority or the word of others. Others called Jesus the Son of God, but Thomas—after the resurrected Jesus appears to him—is the one disciple who calls Jesus "my God."

Once the love of Jesus has overcome us, like Thomas, we are willing to follow Jesus into our death. We are willing to lay down our life (our faith in self) for the sake of others by means of our faith in God as Divine Love in human form. Once we have seen that all true life, freedom, love, and joy belong solely to the Lord of Love, we can clearly see and embrace that the self is an empty vessel.

All good is of God is a truth that becomes a cornerstone of our way of viewing reality. Many of us have tried to be good. We imagine that we can be a "good" person. But this is part of the confusion and delusion of selfhood. Every person whom I consider wise has given up the effort of trying to be good. While all kinds of problems exist in their hearts, they all have learned to accept this fact. They are at peace and raised up away from that inner hell, like Lazarus was lifted to Abraham's bosom in heaven. There is a great gulf that protects them from having to act out the greedy selfishness of their heart. More than most, they know themselves to be but empty vessels, completely dependent on God's mercy and grace.

Along the way of the spiritual journey, God gives us states of joy, peace, and love. We feel freed from the oppression of faith in self. But frequently we quickly slip back into the delusion of self and take credit for the progress. God once healed King Hezekiah of a fatal illness. When Babylonian envoys came to congratulate him on his recovery, he showed them his treasury rather than praising Yahweh. The consequence was the Babylonian conquest of Israel.

In the story from the Gospel of Luke, the greedy rich man wanted Lazarus to convince his five brothers of the reality of afterlife and its nature. Lazarus told him that they cannot be convinced. If the uncaring glutton represents our faith in self, perhaps his five brothers represent that which gives rise to our sense of self: the five senses. It is from the fact that we live in a body, separate and unique in space-time, that our sense of self, individuality, and autonomy arises. We never escape the fact that our five senses cause us to feel as if we are autonomous and individual. Jesus says that unbelievers can't be convinced of the truth even were one to rise from the dead. When we place faith in self below the great gulf—the emptiness of self—our consciousness is liberated with Lazarus up into God's love.

The only thing that makes it to heaven is that which is of God. Jesus says, "No one has ascended into heaven except the one who descended from heaven, the Son of Man" (John 3:13). We are blessed to be emptiness because into that emptiness God can enter, dwell, and animate. When God does this, we feel his ineffable gifts: joy, peace, and goodwill toward all life as if it were our own.

We need not wait to die physically for the tables to be turned between the rich man and the Lazarus within, but we must die to faith in the self. Self is not bad. On the contrary, the sense of self is the matrix from which we are able to exist and participate in the dance of Divine Love. Faith in the self is what leads to trouble. The sensation of selfhood is perhaps the most consistent and convincing illusion we have. When God's will animates us, when it shapes our thoughts and so our actions, we feel free and alive as if on our own. We retain a sense of self. We give of "ourselves" to others and we rejoice in their joy and growth. We feel more alive and happy and independent than ever before.

It is a blessing that we retain the sense of selfhood; without it we could not exist. Without a sense of self, we'd have no consciousness. Were we absorbed into a universal oneness, "other" would no longer exist. Without other, there is nothing to relate to, nothing to communicate with, and nothing to love. Everything would cease to exist. So the illusion of selfhood is in fact one of God's greatest tricks and greatest gifts. It allows us to participate in his life. But the blessing of sense of self is only realized in context of the truth that there is no self.

The shortest verse of the Bible is contained in this story: "Jesus wept." A few verses prior we read Jesus saying that he's glad Lazarus died so that the disciples might believe. It seems likely he is weeping because of his love for others; he feels the pain of those around him. He can see the big picture, but others, including Martha and Mary, cannot.

In both of the Lazarus stories, Lazarus dies. In both stories, I understand Lazarus to symbolize our self-based effort to resist selfishness, to be spiritual beings. This aspect of our being is described as poor and weak. The death of Lazarus represents the moment we despair of our own power to be good. The rich man, who also dies in that parable, represents our selfishness. Just as the death of Lazarus is immediately followed by the death of the rich man, so the death of hope in our own spiritual capacities is paradoxically followed by our release into new freedom from our selfishness. Twelve-step programs are founded on this paradox—in admitting our powerlessness, we suddenly find God's power.

Jesus speaks of this paradox elsewhere:

Strive to enter through the narrow door; for many, I tell you, will try to enter and will not be able. When once the owner of the house has got up and shut the door, and you begin to stand outside and to knock at the door, saying "Lord, open to us," then in reply he will say to you, "I do not know where you come from." Then you will begin to say, "We ate and drank with you, and you taught in our streets." But he will say, "I do not know where you come from; go away from me, all you evildoers!" There will be weeping and gnashing of teeth when you see Abraham and Isaac and Jacob and all the prophets in the kingdom of God, and you yourselves thrown out. Then people will come from the east and west, from north and south, and will eat in the kingdom of God. Indeed, some are last who will be first, and some are first who will be last. (Luke 13:24–30)

On first reading these words seem to suggest that we have to try really hard and just maybe we may be among the select few who actually get into heaven. However, deeper analysis and meditation on these words reveal that this is unlikely to be the message. I believe these words actually are Jesus's way of, first, motivating us toward embarking on the spiritual journey, and then describing to us—warning us, really—about what this journey will entail. The motivation comes in two forms—his urging that we strive to enter the narrow gate is the first. The second is the fact that a cursory understanding of this passage appears to indicate stiff competition.

I don't believe this passage is actually talking about a salvation ratio. I believe this passage is describing the process by which we arrive in the heavenly state of mind. First, we must strive hard to "enter through the narrow door," which is to say, be good and loving. What I have personally found is that despite my utmost efforts to be loving and live according to God's ways, I fall far short of the mark. I find myself on the outside saying, "Please let me in! I was a dedicated servant, a friend." It is true, I tried. But judging from my thoughts, attitudes, and behaviors, I certainly can't say I succeeded in entering that narrow gate.

So this is the process by which God whittles away at my arrogance. It is the process of showing me my spiritual poverty until finally I give up the ghost. I realize I'm last. But in this God-given realization, I am lifted up. "Some are last who will be first, and some are first who will be last." Again, this isn't explaining who goes to heaven and who to hell. Rather it is explaining how we get to heaven, which entails first experiencing our personal hell. Only after recognizing our hell are we able to be given heaven. If we were given it beforehand, we'd take credit for the blessing as if we earned it, or deserved it, or were given it because of our inherent specialness, or because we are chosen. It is true, we are chosen and elected to heaven by Divine Love, but so is everyone else. If Divine Love decides to save even one empty and powerless vessel, then by the nature of Divine Love, all must be likewise saved.

A part of us, like Thomas, is willing to follow Jesus's mission of love despite the fact that we are required to lay down our life for the sake of others. As the above message about the narrow door and the parable of Lazarus explain, attempting to follow the Lord actually produces two deaths. The first death is that of the Lazarus in the Gospel of John, who represents our ability to be selfless, loving, and caring human beings. Though Jesus, the Divine, sees the big picture and is "glad for our sakes" that this death is occurring, from within our human experience of the death, we mourn. Mary and Martha represent our utter despair and sorrow in relation to our complete spiritual death. We are so dead spiritually that we stink. It's been four days—beyond hope for recovery. We have to hit that kind of rock bottom. We have to reach a profound sense of despair. And unfortunately, just knowing that such despair is a part of the process doesn't allow us to evade the process. We may, like Thomas and the other disciples, understand the process intellectually. But when it comes to the emotions of our heart, we have to feel the despair just as fully as those who haven't been clued in to the process of becoming a loving person and so coming to know joy and peace. Like Mary and Martha, we will mourn.

Martha and Mary both express their simultaneous faith and despair in like manner, "Lord, if you had been here, my brother would not have died." Jesus assures them: "I am the resurrection and the life. Those who believe in me, even though they die, will live, and everyone who lives and believes in me will never die. Do you believe this?" This is an amazing question. Do we really believe that in Jesus is resurrection and life? Do we even know what these things mean? Jesus later says, "Did I not tell you that if you believed, you would see the glory of God?" As has been true in many of the miracles, it can only occur if we believe.

If we have arrived at this point in our journey, however, and come to see that yes, of our self, we are utterly lifeless, then I believe, like Martha, we will respond affirmatively: *Yes, Lord, I believe that you are the Savior, the Christ of God.* I believe that God will only expose us to our spiritual death after we have spent effort trying to enter that narrow gate. The failed effort is what causes us to realize that we are dead. And if we don't believe in Jesus, in Love as a real living God, higher and more human than our own being, then we will not have made the effort. So by the time we get to this agonizing moment, we have already invested our life into the message and way of Jesus, of Love as Divine. We have nothing left. We know we are dead. We can do nothing but throw ourselves on our Lord in utter despair and weeping. Yes, I believe.

Jesus wept. In this miracle moment, our weeping, because it is of Love, is Jesus's weeping. This moment where the heart of a woman (Martha) and the heart of God resonate as one is the moment in which God has secretly replaced our dead heart with his living heart. Our weeping is of God's love. I believe the moment Jesus wept is the moment that Lazarus—our spiritual life—was resurrected. Note that Jesus then thanks the Father for having already heard him. This supports the idea that Lazarus had already been resurrected before the stone was removed. Our despair is God's life-giving love resurrected within us, but within the despair we are not yet aware. The state of despair is the means of our resurrection.

Jesus next instructs the stone to be rolled away. Within our despair, we don't yet realize that God's love has been given into our hearts as our own. It is ironically that very despair that is God's love. The removal of the stone and Jesus's prayer speak to the moment we begin to intellectually understand that God is resurrecting us to spiritual life. "Father, I thank you for having heard me. I know that you always hear me, but I have said this for the sake of the crowd standing here, so that they may believe that you sent me." Jesus knows the big picture, but he chooses the right moment to fill us in. The Father is Yahweh. Yahweh means *I Am That I Am*. This implies self-existent being, the source of all reality. Here Jesus says that he knows the Father always hears and responds positively to his requests. In other words, reality always is propelled and guided by the voice and desire of Love. So complete is this equation that Love is Reality and Reality is Love. "I and the Father are One," says Jesus in John 10:30. "If you know me, you will know my Father also" (John 14:9). God can see that Love and Reality are one, but our human perception lags far behind. This moment—when the stone is removed and Jesus prays that the people might also understand that the Father works in concert with the will of the Son—indicates the moment in which we begin to perceive for ourselves that all of reality is in fact the ever-opening self-revelation of pure Divine Love. We exist as participants in the joy-dance of Divine Love.

Jesus then commands, "Lazarus, come out!" All are astounded as Lazarus comes out of the cave. Jesus instructs that the grave clothes be removed. Now that we fully believe and understand that our spiritual life, our power, comes entirely from the Lord, we are given to exercise power for good as if it were our own. I believe that this is the process by which grace and mercy enter into our lives and heal us.

Jesus tells us that he is the vine and we the branches. It is his life that lives in us, and this is the life that is saved. We observe his love and even feel it within us exactly as if it were our own love. We rejoice to see the joy of our loved ones and that joy feels as if it is our own. But we know from past experience that that is not our love, nor is it our joy. It is God's. What is our own is nothing but delusion and the hell of living from delusion. We are empty. But God, somehow, infuses his living love and joy so perfectly into our consciousness that we feel as if we are alive and that we are living beings with separate entities. But Jesus prayed, "The glory that you have given me I have given them, so that they may be one, as we are one, I in them and you in me, that they may become completely one" (John 17:22–23).

We are of the one, because only the one is real and has life. Somehow, miraculously and beyond my ability to understand, I seem to be alive and I have a consciousness that seems separate and unique to me. I don't know how this works. And I don't care. I am grateful to have life. I am grateful too for my sense of separateness and individuality. I mentioned that the delusion of selfhood is a blessing when tempered with the knowledge of our fundamental emptiness. The blessing of the persistent and perfect illusion of self is that we are able to love and be loved. And that is heaven. So what is it that goes to heaven? Really it is Jesus, God. Jesus says, "I am the resurrection and the life." He also says, "This is eternal life, that they may know you, the only true God, and Jesus Christ whom you have sent" (John 17:3). He also says to Nicodemus that no one enters heaven except the one who comes down from heaven, namely God himself. In other words, our sense of self, when united to an acknowledgment of the emptiness of self, is able to experience heavenly joy, love, and peace.

At the end of the Bible, the beautiful, wonderful city New Jerusalem is described. Twelve gemstones stand as the foundation of its walls. Twelve pearls serve as gates opening up to its peace and wondrous beauty. Its streets are paved with pure gold, "as clear as glass" (Rev. 21:18). Nothing of evil or of deceit may enter its gates. It is a place of perpetual light, the pure light of "The Lord God Almighty and the Lamb" (Rev. 21:22) who are its temple. Within it is a river of life flowing clear as crystal, and within and all around the river is the tree of life yielding perpetual fruit, whose leaves heal the nations of all diseases. Only those written in the book of life shall enter into this city. There is no death, no disease, no curse, no sorrow, no crying in this city. It is a city of perfect balance between nature and human endeavor. Within these walls, humans love and respect natural beauty, preserving its purity, and nature does no harm to humans.

The more we come to know The Word of God, the more our eyes open up to see the wondrous, brilliant white light of God. We see God's life within the stories, life that is the light of man. Our thoughts become like crystals, catching, reflecting, and shining back the light of God. These thoughts serve as the gemstone foundation of our new life.

But we notice that the living of them doesn't come so fast. Our persistent sense of self and consequent selfish desires arise and disturb us like a grain of sand within an oyster. Year after year, we attempt to align our actions with God's will, and in the process notice our serious shortcomings. From this we gain deeper and deeper insight about our inherent emptiness and need for God. And this— our attempt to do God's will, always tainted with a grain of selfishness—becomes a pearl through which we finally can enter God's peace and love. From our death, God brings life. From a grain of sand, the pearl is made. All the pain, trials, and temptations of life turn out to be the stuff by which we grow and are able to enter into a heavenly state of mind. We enter through the pearl of our experience, strength, and hope.

Once inside this celestial state of mind, we find that new avenues open up between us and those around us. Our hearts are filled with that heavenly gold we know as love, and that goodwill unites us with others like broad, well-lit streets. Inside the city is the throne of God. God's throne of judgment issues forth but one judgment: "I, your God, love you forever and ever." And from that throne issues forth a pure, living river of water clear as crystal. From this fundamental truth, that God loves us, we gain access to all kinds of truths that clean us, that quench our thirst for knowledge and wisdom. It is such a full and pure wisdom that it is as if our spirit is actually immersed, swimming and playing within the joyful good news of God's love and mercy for us.

In and on both sides of the river, a tree rises up strong and full of fruit: the tree of life. We see how the human race, all the lives of the human race, meld together to become one tree of life in the context of God's love. We are bound to all others in love. The love that God is able to express through us reaches out to others and affects them for good. They in turn spread that love. In fact, it is amplified as it continues through time. It keeps expanding forever. Imagine that Jesus was like a rock dropped into the pool of human life. His life caused ripples that are growing and changing all human beings, now and forever. His love will never die; it keeps expanding, and it finds expression in us and through us. It turns out that we as individuals aren't alive, but his love, which reaches out through us and weaves us together, is alive. This unites us all. That is the tree of life. We are but cells of a much larger and more living Life.

The leaves of that tree are for the healing of the nations. When we hear the honest experience, strength, and hope of other individuals created out of their individual journey toward God, we are blessed and are able to grow. The honest stories of other people serve to heal us. The fruit of the tree is always available and plentiful throughout the year. It is this form of God's living love expressed within the human race that gives rise to that which feeds our souls. Deep inside, we all long to be connected and unite to others. Jesus said that doing the will of God is his food. So it is with us. When God's will is expressed in our actions of love, we feel united to God and others, and we are fed deeply and satisfyingly.

We have seen that our minds are like a nation of people. Myriads of spiritual forces are constantly flowing through us. Our sense of self latches onto these desires and loves, imagining them to be who we are. But none of these "me"s can enter the city. Those who are in the book of life and are saved represent those states of mind that know the truth of our inherent emptiness and utter need for God; those states that love God with holy, grateful awe. God fills these states of mind with his light, a light that doesn't fade.

I want to look at a story about one of Solomon's judgments because it seems to be a perfect analogy for the dilemma of the idea of an eternal hell. Two mothers were both claiming a single male child. Solomon ordered the child to be cut into two pieces. One woman agreed to the decree, but the other cried out that she was willing to give the baby up. From this woman's love, Solomon then knew her to be the rightful mother.

Let's think of the human race as the baby boy of the story. In the story, the judgment of the king is to divide the male child into two pieces. We can see this judgment also in mainstream Christian thought—some members of the human race go to heaven while others go to hell. Indeed, many verses in the Bible seem to support this idea. It would not be difficult to draw a convincing argument from the Word that many human beings are cast into hell and suffer for all of eternity.

I have never been comfortable with this verdict, for several reasons. First, as mentioned above, our virtue cannot be ascribed to our own being, but to God alone. This includes not only our works, but our faith and the good impulses of our hearts. So any person in heaven would instantly say they do not deserve to be there.

Likewise, selfish impulses arise from this convincing delusion of selfhood, which in turn arise from the five senses. Without God's mercy and blessing, none of us would ever be able to rise above the delusion of self-autonomy or the selfish impulses that it induces. We are all doomed to the hellish isolation of self-obsession and sin except for the grace of God. And no one of us deserves that grace any more than the next. So if it were the case that some of us went to heaven and others to hell, it would mean that God is completely arbitrary and, in fact, unjust. I can't believe in an arbitrary, unjust God.

The second reason I don't feel comfortable with the idea of the eternal division of the human race—one to suffering, the other to grace—is that love can't abide this result. To be raised into heaven while a loved one is cast to hell is no reward, no eternity of bliss. Quite the opposite—it is suffering for all. Those who supposedly make it to heaven will no doubt have a large measure of God's mercy and compassion, sympathy and empathy. So the pain of those suffering in hell is felt all the more acutely by those in heaven. It just doesn't work.

And finally, I can't see how the God of infinite wisdom and unfathomable love would arrange for a system in which a large portion of his beloved children end up in hell because they were deluded by the very convincing impulses of the senses and sense of self that arise from our corporal housing. I'm quite sure he wouldn't have set such a universe in motion.

So I stand with the woman in Solomon's court who relinquishes her child, rather than have it killed. I relinquish my claim to an orthodox faith and so my chance for heaven. I admit that the Bible indicates an eternal heaven for some and an eternal hell for others; nevertheless, I don't believe it to be true. After a lifetime of thinking about this very issue, I feel that I've glimpsed the hidden verdict within the apparent verdict. The human race is God's baby, his beloved baby. The apparent message that this baby is to be divided is a test of sorts. It is a method of drawing out an important step in our spiritual awakening. God is prompting us to look at the verdict and say, "No! I'd rather go to hell myself than to believe in a God that sends many to hell." God wants us to rebel against this apparent judgment just as the woman did in the story. And then God's true verdict is revealed: it is not individuals cast into the fiery lake never again to escape, but our selfish, hateful, deceptive, and lustful states of mind. These will be divided from us.

God will not throw the baby out with the bathwater. And indeed, even the most destructive human beings to have walked the earth have all started out in the same way—as a tiny, helpless, and innocent baby. They began life in need of spiritual nourishment and training. They needed love and guidance. Somehow, they didn't get what they needed. But what happens to that tiny baby, that lonely child? Those states of mind of youth are still stored and are incorporated as aspects of the adult. That child, that infant, can't be cast into hell simply because it is inexorably incorporated into the mind of the adult sinner. No, I'm quite sure that after a purification and awakening process, some aspect of our beings is raised into heaven.

If we truly believe, as is the case, that all goodness and all power to believe and do good comes from the Lord of Love alone, then it makes no sense to believe that some humans "choose" hell while others "choose" heaven. It makes even less sense to believe that the Lord of Love predestines some of his beloved children for heaven and others for hell. I believe in predestination—universal predestination to a heaven of mercy.

For me, believing that some aspect of all of us will eventually arrive in heaven is also practically useful. When I believe that the end of the story of life is good, not just for a few, but for all of us, a great deal of anxiety is relieved. And as fears leave, peace and goodwill take their place. I am better able to relate to people, accept people for who they are and so love them, when I believe in an eternally good plan for all of us. In fact, on rare occasions, when God lifts me up for a better view, knowing that the future is heavenly allows me to see the here and now—no matter how ugly, challenging, or ill it may seem—as an aspect of that heaven. The belief in eternal heaven for all improves me. As Jesus says, "a tree is known by its fruit," which to me means that ideas are as good as the effects they produce. Universal salvation is an idea that, in my opinion, produces the good fruit of goodwill and consequent action. The adventure of life on earth, with its pain and pleasure, suffering and joy, exists for the sake of the eventual eternal joy of all people. Without a temporal experience of suffering, we have no ability to sense, understand, or rejoice in the opposite of suffering—eternal joy.

We don't need to die physically to enter the promised land. The kingdom of heaven is within. It is here and now, waiting for us. But that foundation of crystalline, true ideas that catch God's shining light must be laid down firmly and strongly within us. We must put in the effort of overcoming our sense of self with the truth of our emptiness, and we do this not so much with thought, but through action. We must daily take up our cross and allow our sense of self to die to prove the verity of our faith. Day in, day out, our efforts to walk as Jesus would have us walk, our failures and our successes, create the pearl of wisdom that serves as the entrance to a heavenly state of mind.

The more we actively try to walk as Jesus would have us, the more we awaken to our shortcomings and selfishness. And then we realize that God is working his miracle of resurrection within our lives. We are dead, but we feel alive, truly alive. We are full of joy and love. We feel free to love. We feel awake to God's life shimmering within nature, others, and events. We see that problems and evils are means to an end, parts of the pearls that are the gates of heaven. We see the truth of what Jesus says, that the pains and troubles of this world are just birth pains, and we are being born into heavenly reality.

In relation to his second coming to earth, Christ assured us "I am coming soon" (Rev. 3:11). It's been two thousand years. That doesn't seem very quick. He even told his disciples that he'd come before some of them had died. Jesus said that there'd be a lot of calamity and trouble just before he arrives, descending within the clouds of glory to judge the nations. Perhaps we're looking for him in the wrong way. Just as the Jews were taken by surprise at Yahweh's first manifestation, it seems quite possible that we might be surprised at his second.

What if we look at all of this in terms not of the worldly realm, but the terrain of our spirit. After we go through a lot of hell, the predicted times of calamity, we'll see the beautiful truth about God and his love descending into our minds. Those thoughts are the clouds of glory—nice, but not enough. But as he said, he's coming soon. Those thoughts will come down and reach earth, that is, they will alter the way we live. Our actions will begin to communicate the love of God, rather than the love of self. Now Yahweh has again become "God-With-Us," quite literally.

The second coming of Christ isn't something for which to wait, but to live. The glory of the true ideas about God, residing in our thoughts like clouds, descend and become the living, truly human life of God within us. Jesus said that he would divide the nations, casting the evil into hell and the good into heaven. And he does divide the inner nations, the good from the bad. He does cast all the bad ways of thinking and being into an eternity of hell—thank goodness for that! It is his greatest mercy. When Jesus says that he saves us from sin, it doesn't mean that we can sin and not suffer in hell. It means that when we get to know him, love him, and let his life live out in our actions, we won't have to sin anymore. It's not a matter of faith, but of fact.

When Jesus came the first time the angel announced, "Peace on earth and goodwill toward all human beings." Sometimes I've wondered, *whatever happened to that nice ideal?* But now I see its fulfillment. It isn't a false promise. Those wise, and for the most part old, men and women I know who have been through the wringer and birth pains of life exhibit both of these qualities. They have peace within themselves and they have goodwill not just toward some, but toward all people. Jesus has made his second coming in their hearts.

So be of good cheer. He is truly coming soon.

MEDITATIONS

1. After entering into a meditative state, blank your mind completely. Rather than visualizing anything, try to experience your lack of spiritual life by keeping your mind completely blank. Most of us initially experience concerns of the day crowding into the empty mind. However, with concerted effort and practice, most people can persevere and enter into an exquisitely peaceful and blissful state of mind. What you will likely experience is that into that empty stillness comes God. When our minds are preoccupied with thoughts, God's palpable presence is kept at bay. Once we completely quiet our minds, however, we will come to feel God's presence with us and we will realize that he has been there all along.

2. Imagine that you are Lazarus. Feel yourself sicken and weaken

as your family worries. Your sisters tell you that they have sent word to Jesus. He will come. He will heal you. But your strength fades, and you cannot hold on any longer. Darkness closes around you. Your sense of self is collapsing. Remain in this state of emptiness of self for some time.

Suddenly you awake. It is still dark, and something is wrapped around you, keeping you from moving. You fight your way free, wondering where you are. There is a loud noise and a blinding light as a stone is rolled away from in front of you. You walk into the light, feeling the sun warm your body, feeling life flow through your veins. Your bonds fall off. You see your sisters running to embrace you. The love you feel in this moment is heaven. The surroundings and people are the same, but your heart and mind are completely new.

Now, back in your own personality and life, spend time focusing on your loved ones. Bring them to mind with blessing and gratitude. Do the same for all the blessings of nature. Focus with gratitude on the beauty of the skies—the stars, the moon, the sun, the clouds. Focus on the gift of water, ascending and descending, running down the mountains and across the lands with its clear joy. Focus on the wonder of the trees and flowers and all the blessings the vegetable kingdom offers us. Focus on the grace and freedom of the birds. Focus on the mystery of marine life. Praise and thank God for all that is. Recognize that it is the ever-opening flower of divine love and joy. Heaven is here and now in all life. Once we die to self and awaken to the understanding of love as the Lord, we are allowed to drink in the life of heaven.

LEAVES

1. God begins to resurrect us to a heavenly state of mind only when we despair.

2. Despair is God's love living in us in the absence of God's perspective.

3. That love is our resurrection.

4. Reality is the expression of Love's dictation.

5. When we see that all things are orchestrated by love for the sake of the salvation of all, the stone is rolled away and we are alive spiritually.

FRUIT

1. Practice one of the above meditations every day.

2. Try living one day from the perspective that each and every person you encounter is an angel in the making, an expression of God's loving work. If you like the experience, keep at it.

3. Do something out of the ordinary to express and share the joy inherent in the idea that we are all loved and saved by Jesus, the Lord of Love. You may want to prepare a feast for your family or friends. You may want to offer your help at a local charity. You may want to write a letter to an old friend or even an old enemy.

4. Write down all doubting thoughts that counter the idea that the Lord alone saves and the idea of universal salvation. Look at each one and write down what you gain from it. Imagine what life would be like for you without those thoughts. Decide which you prefer.

DISCUSSION QUESTIONS

1. What did you find useful from the chapter?

2. How did this week's daily meditation affect you?

3. Did you notice any important changes in your life this week?

4. Have you had an experience of spiritual despair? What happened next?

5. Were you able to experience spiritual emptiness? If so, what was it like? Do you find yourself resisting the idea? If so, why?

6. What do you think of the idea expressed in this chapter that there is no permanent division of the human race into heaven and hell, that we are all destined for heaven? Do you find the idea of certain people being consigned to hell satisfying? Why or why not?

7. Please share any other insights that you've gained over the course of the week.

APPENDIX

MEDITATION

What is the meditative state of mind like?

It is like a leaf upon a gently flowing stream.

It is like being atop a mountain, above all the usual activities of the day.

It is like discovering a secret door out of the cluttered house of normal consciousness into a wonderful free land of rich promise.

It is like an eagle soaring above the valley below.

Through meditation, we enter into a state of being that is higher than the sense of self derived from normal waking consciousness. Much of the time, we are caught up in what we do, think, feel, and want. At these times, we fail to realize that while our consciousness enters into these things, it is not bound by them. Once we have equated our selfhood with these things, we are in a sense imprisoned by them. If, for example, we begin to feel depressed, we may so identify with these emotions that we believe life to be worthless. Or if we fail to realize that we can rise above the various desires we feel, we may find ourselves trapped in a cycle of compulsive behavior. Sometimes we enjoy a certain amount of control over our thoughts. At other times, however, we may be plagued with negative or obsessive thinking from which we cannot extricate ourselves under normal circumstances. We must find a form of consciousness that is beyond the grasp of these thoughts, these negative emotions, these self-serving and destructive desires. Meditation liberates the mind and sense of self from such prisons.

In the stillness of meditation, consciousness rises above the normal concerns and preoccupations of the day. We discover that our true self transcends our body, feelings, thoughts, and desires. We come home to our true and highest nature. This experience is characterized by a state of freedom, pervasive peace, bliss, appreciation, and unconditional love. Thus the less we are attached to our individuality—personal thoughts, desires, emotions, and the body—the more truly alive we feel. For this reason we intuitively come to know through meditation that our true vitality and existence is inherently united with that of all others, with life and God himself. We experience unity with all and we experience that this is our truest nature. Thus we come to know that our individuality is an appendage of our true life, which is also the same true life within all that exists. He is the vine, we are the branches. As Jesus prayed, we are one in him. Thus, in the meditative state, consciousness is less grounded within the things of earth, and is touching upon the things of spirit. Our consciousness is learning to fly.

Jesus says to Nicodemus that no one can enter heaven except he who came down from heaven. In meditation, we are not entering heaven. Rather, we are putting to sleep all those forms of consciousness that arise from earth and so are unable to enter heaven. God is Spirit. I believe that the possibilities for what can happen as a result of this tapping into the realm of spirit, into God, are boundless. The world of spirit is bound by neither space nor time. We will be increasingly attuned to the spiritual and psychological needs of others. We will have intuitions and insights into the future. We will find ourselves empowered and emboldened to serve where we once would have shied away. And we will know that it isn't our "self" that is able to do these things. It is our awakening to the transcendent realm of spirit that enables such experiences to occur.

Though the meditative experience is special, enlivening, and wondrous, it is not the goal. It is the means. The goal is to bring the experience to bear on our day-to-day activities here on earth. The goal is to become kinder, gentler, wiser, and more productive in the work of love. We have been given a space- and time-derived sense of self for a reason, namely, to celebrate Divine Love with one another. We gather the joy and confidence of love while meditating and then bring it down into our interactions in such a way as to bless others and increase the presence of Divine Love on earth. In word, we meditate to help make the Lord's kingdom "on earth, as it is in heaven."

For the soul who practices meditation regularly, there will likely be powerful experiences. However, often the awakening of which I speak is subtle. There may be many days where nothing much seems to be happening. The operative word is "seems." Even when we don't sense any awakening, the practice of meditating, when done in earnest, is changing us for the better. As in any discipline, not every day is a performance day, full of glory and fun. We practice so that on the day of the big game, recital, or show, we are prepared. My experience is that God decides when the powerful experiences unfold. My job is to persist in the practice. And admittedly, I am not always good at this. Because I believe loving activity in the world is the ultimate goal, I sometimes allow activity to eclipse my practicing of meditation. When I do, it is a matter of time before my emotions, thoughts, desires, and behaviors spin out of control. A return to the practice of meditation always has powerful effects in re-centering me. Even when I don't perceive the powerful sense of awakening, the practice itself is having unnoticed stabilizing effects in my life.

OVERCOMING THREE
HURDLES TO MEDITATION
Distrust

I have encountered people who are wary of meditating, suspicious that it is some kind of magical art or somehow otherwise un-Christian. However, the word meditation simply means concentration. The meditative state is one in which the mind is undistracted and focused. And in the case of this book, we are accessing this meditative state of mind for the sake of entering profoundly into the Word of God. David, the Psalmist, writes about meditating on his bed and meditating on the Law of God. We read that Isaac was meditating in the field when Rebecca, his bride to be, was approaching for the first time. I like this image very much as an analogy for meditation. When we meditate, it is as if our mind finds its true soul partner for the first time. We feel completed, whole, and where we are supposed to be.

It seems very possible that on the occasions when Jesus withdrew from the crowds into the wilderness, he spent this alone time meditating. Deep prayer is in fact a form of meditation in that the mind is very focused. However, other forms of meditation might be considered a focusing of the mind onto listening to God, rather than speaking to God, as in the case of prayer. We still our mind of our own thoughts so as to be open and receptive to messages from a source higher than ourselves, God.

Impatience

The second major hurdle that may prevent us from meditating regularly is impatience. Developing the practice of meditation takes time and effort, just like all other valuable skills in life. In the early stages, many of us find our minds to be completely unruly and seemingly untamable. We sit down to meditate and rather than the sense of peace we expect, our thoughts race away about trivial future concerns or memories from the past. However, persistence will move us beyond this stage. If we persevere, we will begin to experience the joy of meditating.

If we continue in the practice, it is likely we enter a period in which we feel tedium and boredom. I once read a joke that said something along the lines of, "My son used to sit around and do nothing . . . now he meditates." The joke implies that meditating is sitting around and doing nothing. We may encounter internal messages such as, *Wouldn't my time be better spent actually doing something?*

However, though the body is not moving, to meditate is to be participating in a profoundly useful activity. What could be more important than increasing our inner sense of peace and gratitude? What is more valuable than discovering a deeply intimate and real sense of God's presence in our lives? I believe that meditation improves mental agility, clarity, creativity, intuition, emotional peace, spiritual awareness, and physical health. These gifts carry over into all of the activities we engage in throughout the rest of the day. When we feel as if our practice of meditation is useless or a waste of time, we can recall that we are in fact doing something of the utmost importance because it positively influences all of our other activities. When we are more centered as a result of meditation, we will respond to those around us in more healthy and healing ways. Our relationships will improve. Our spiritual productivity will blossom in that we will increasingly be a positive channel of God's love here on earth.

Sense of Intimidation

The prospect of meditating can be daunting. The mystique often associated with meditation leaves some people feeling dubious about its practice and others intimidated. Fortunately, while the experience of meditation can indeed be profound and transcendent, the practice is not complicated; on the contrary, it is simple. I like to think of the meditating mind as a bird in flight. Though the bird's activity of moving her wings up and down is not complicated, the result of this activity yields the wonderfully liberating experience of flight. In the same way, the simple practice of meditation can have magnificent results. And similar to flight, meditating requires practice and the strengthening of mental "muscles." If you are concerned that you may not have what it takes to meditate, I encourage you lay down those fears. You don't have to understand how to fly or even what flight is; all you have to do is practice flapping the wings. With practice, your mind will enter a state of meditation. You will discover and enter into a state proper to your being the same way a bird discovers flight to be proper to its form. Your mind has come into its own. Below I will describe a few simple techniques for initiating a meditative state of mind.

THE PROCESS OF MEDITATION

Induction: Preparatory Yoga/Stretches

I have found that engaging in a short five-minute, yoga-like routine consistently leads to an increase in clarity and depth of meditation. Going through the stretches and postures serves to signal and prepare the mind for meditation. It also releases tensions stored in the body and so produces a physical state of peace corresponding to the meditative peace to follow. When I do this short yoga routine, I consider it a form of non-verbal prayer. I try not to think thoughts at this time, but simply be in my body and let my body be the communication. The process is as follows:

1. I begin lying down on my stomach, allowing this to be a communication of my spiritual lack of life and need for God. I arch my back until my straight arms are holding me in a cobra-like position.

2. I then move to a kneeling position with a straight back, allowing this posture to represent a request for God to be with me.

3. I then rise up to a standing position with arms and hands stretched up wide and high. I enter into the message of this position, which for me is one of gratitude and praise.

4. I then begin to slowly arch backwards. When I can go no farther without falling, I kneel and then continue to arch backwards until my head and shoulders are resting on the floor with lower legs tucked under the thighs. This is a very uncomfortable position, but it does stretch out and relax the thighs and torso. For me, this position is a communication of the fact that God's mercy and presence are overpowering and beyond what I can fathom or handle.

5. I then bring my legs to a straight position so that I am lying flat on my back. This position communicates the peace of confidence in God's loving plans.

6. I then draw my legs and hips up, so that my toes are pointing toward the sky and I support my hips with my hands, using my elbows as braces on the floor. This position reminds me of a sprouting seed and so for me is a communication of spiritual growth and beginnings.

7. I then bring my straightened legs over my head until my toes are touching the floor above my head. This is also a very uncomfortable position and for me communicates a state of spiritual battle and temptation.

8. I then slowly uncurl my back until I am again lying on my back and enjoy the sensation of great physical and mental peace that ensues.

This routine need not be used, but I offer it as an option. I do, however, recommend getting out of your thoughts and into your body while doing stretches of some kind as a way of preparing and signally your mind for a time of meditation.

Creating a Physical Space

It is also beneficial to have a special place to practice meditation—a place that is used exclusively for meditating. After developing a regular practice within your chosen space, just drawing near the space will bring you a sense of peace and contentment. It will truly become a special space of solace. The space itself will then help you enter into a meditative state of mind. You may wish to adorn this space with objects of beauty and special meaning in your life.

Routine and Duration

I have more than once read authors advising meditating for set amounts of time at set times of day. In truth, I cannot comment on this because I have never practiced in this way. It makes sense that this recommendation would be a good idea, but my particular character seems to have an allergy to routine and schedule! I try to meditate at least once a day but at no particular time. I generally stop meditating when I sense a natural recall from the meditative state. Perhaps I would benefit from pressing on beyond this sense of natural closure, however, as I have not often done so, I cannot comment on this. Twenty to forty minutes is the amount of time I generally find to have lapsed while meditating.

Posture

I am not qualified to make a definitive statement about the importance of posture; all I can offer is my thoughts on the matter. As I described above in the section on yoga and stretching, I believe that every position of body is an expression, a communication. The communication of our posture is received not only by others who see us, but also by our own minds, and I believe it cannot help but influence how we think and feel. Since the mind is that aspect of our being which receives the things of spirit, it makes sense that posture, having influence on our own mind, does have some influence on what will occur when we meditate.

In my mind, however, there are only two essential ingredients to the meditative posture. First, it is important that you not be so comfortable that you fall asleep. I have had no success meditating while lying down, but it might be right for you. Emanuel Swedenborg, a Christian mystic of the eighteenth century who had profound and extensive spiritual experiences, would meditate hours on end while lying down.

The second essential ingredient of meditative posture, as I see it, is that it not be too painful or harmful. My knees hurt significantly when I sit in a lotus position or even a half-lotus position. Therefore, I sit cross-legged with my backside on my meditation cushion. In my mind, this position communicates peaceful, spiritual receptivity. I usually place the pillow against a wall and keep my back flat up against the wall. Purists might say it is better to keep one's spine straight without the aid of a wall. I fold the corner of the cushion up so that my bum is higher than my crossed legs. I have heard of some meditators using extra pillows to raise their bums up considerably higher than their knees and ankles so as to relieve strain and pain. Some might prefer to sit in a straight-backed chair with their feet on the floor. This is great. Find what works best and stick with it. I fold my right hand within my left while meditating. Again, I don't think the exact position is essential. Find out what feels right for you, and do that. That's what has worked for me!

Initiation

After I have sat down to meditate, I usually like to begin with a few deep breaths. I typically inhale deeply through my nose and hold the breath while counting down slowly from seven to one, then breathe out. I repeat this two times for a total of three cycles. This serves at least two purposes. It signals the mind that meditation is beginning. It also oxygenates the blood. Once the meditative state has been experienced a few times, the deep breathing will become associated with that state of mind and so help initiate the state in subsequent practice. I encourage you to find an initiation breathing ritual that suits you.

THREE MEDITATIVE PRACTICES
"Thank you, Lord" Mantra: A Practice for Beginners and Veterans Alike

Many paths lead to the meditative state of mind. What follows is a practice especially valuable for beginners. It is very simple and particularly effective at drawing the distracted mind repeatedly back into focus. With every inhalation mentally repeat, "Thank you," and with every exhalation, repeat "Lord." When you hear a distracting noise outside, let the "Thank you, Lord," be in reference to the noise . . . what had been a distraction has now become a doorway opening up to gratitude and meditation. More often, the distracting noise will be on the inside. Random thoughts, recollections, worries, and the like will likely vie for your attention as you begin the practice. Regardless of the thought that happens to jockey its way into your consciousness, carry on with the meta-thought "Thank you, Lord." The subtext is, "Thank you, Lord, for the opportunity to see this distracting thought and to nevertheless carry on meditating on you."

What is particularly beautiful about this practice is that even the most wretched and ugly thoughts are bent back into something positive. For a time in my practice, whenever I sat down to meditate, heinous images of twisted violence would start appearing in my mind. I was tempted to quit practicing. Meditation awakens us to aspects of our mind and being that we had never imagined could exist. I believe the best way to deal with this confrontation with our lowest inner hells during meditation is to understand that this is who we would be were it not for the grace and mercy of the Lord. Meditation increasingly causes us to realize that all good present in our lives is from God, and all selfishness is simply a function of delusion—the delusion of selfhood, that is, a failure to understand that all life is God's alone.

So whenever such wretched images reveal themselves to me, I simply continue saying "Thank you" as I inhale and "Lord" as I exhale. This form of meditation is even effective against seemingly overpowering emotional states such as rage, fear, lust, and hopelessness. The repeated prayer of gratitude converts the emotional experience into something positive. *Thank you, Lord, for this chance to rest in you with trust, even as I feel completely overwhelmed by hopelessness.* We need not think through entire sentences such as the one above, we just keep saying "Thank you, Lord," and that gratitude reaches out into all that is occupying our minds and defuses its negative power. It transforms the experience into spiritual progress. All that is required is that we continue sitting, breathing, and mentally repeating, "Thank you, Lord."

One final remarkable benefit of this practice is that it can be brought away from the meditation cushion and into everyday life. I have had some wonderful experiences from greeting all the events and people of a day while mentally repeating, "Thank you, Lord." I wish I remembered to do so more often.

This meditation can be varied. Try "Lord," on the inhalation and "Thank you" on the exhalation. Or try the whole phrase on the exhalation and leave the inhalation blank. You can try the simple but effective phrases "In Lord," and "Out Lord." Each breath is a gift of life from the Divine, and then we give it out again to all around us.

Moving Beyond Verbal Translations of Consciousness

For many of us, consciousness is predominantly focused on verbal thought-forms; so much so that we may equate consciousness with such forms of thought. However, dreams, daydreams, music, and even math are proof that consciousness can operate without the aid of verbal translation. Though clearly useful, verbal forms of thought are contracted and limited. They are directed by our personal sense of will and bind consciousness to time. In the practice described here, the goal is to withdraw the mind from verbal translations and discover a form of consciousness that is consequently less bound to sense of time, self, and linguistic memories. A pet theory of mine is that because we learn to use language as our predominant mode of thinking somewhere in childhood, verbal forms of thinking cannot tap into pre-toddler states of being. In contrast, nonverbal forms of consciousness are not bound by this, and through them we can touch upon preverbal infant states—not so much in the form of memories, but in the form of states of mind and being. By escaping directed, verbal forms of consciousness, we can touch upon the peace, trust, wonder, gentleness, and unselfconscious appreciation that characterize infant states of being.

The practice described here helps us to escape directed and verbal thoughts, releasing us into undirected and nonverbal forms of consciousness. This is a more difficult form of meditation.

Once sitting, and having taken in the initiative breaths, disengage from verbal thought. It is hard to describe how to do this except that you stop thinking. There are a few ways of entering this form of consciousness. One way is to close your eyes and look at the space behind your forehead. Just observe what you see. Another way is to simply experience breathing. Another is rest consciousness in the sensation of the entire body simultaneously—that is, to simply sit and be aware of your physical body. Still another way is to refuse to direct thoughts.

I often find that my breathing stops for several seconds when my mind becomes devoid of verbal thought. I have found it tricky to sustain this state after breathing begins again. However, reverently meditating on the experience of breathing as a gift from the Divine allows breathing to occur without the introduction of verbal thought. Our breathing is God's ever-present communication of his sustaining love for us. Try sitting and becoming absorbed in the delight of the sensation of breathing.

I have found there to be degrees of nonverbal consciousness. Often, there will be a collage of verbal messages floating around in the background. I am only vaguely aware of them. It is similar to the blurry awareness of a conversation taking place between people nearby when falling asleep. I don't sense myself as directing the verbal thoughts and I don't have full awareness of what their messages contain. Going a little deeper into the nonverbal state, a collage of visual images occurs. Faces and all manner of other images appear one after another with seemingly no order or reason. On very rare occasions, I have entered into a state very similar to dream in which there is a meaningful sequence of visual and auditory events that I do not feel to be directing whatsoever. I consider these to be visions. I have always gained a meaningful life lesson from these experiences.

Directed Visual Meditations

Directed visual meditations are the kind of meditation offered at the end of each chapter in this book. They can be very profound or they can be nearly meaningless depending on the depth and focus with which one enters into them. To ensure that this form of meditation is worth the time required, I recommend first entering into a state of meditation using one of the practices described above. Once the mind has been focused and emptied of everyday concerns, the directed visual meditations will be much more effective and moving.

This practice involves having a set idea of what you want to see and do in the visual meditation before sitting down. Once you enter a state of meditation, you mentally move through the pre-scripted experience as vividly as possible, employing all senses mentally as fully as possible. I have found this to be an excellent and very potent way of meditating on the Word of God. This practice opened up my relationship with the Lord in a wonderful way. No longer was the Lord a set of ideas or stories; he became a real person with whom I could interact. There are many applications to this kind of meditation. You can bring an ailing (physically or psychologically) loved one to the Lord and have the Lord embrace or bless him or her. You can ask questions about direction or meaning and receive answers— sometimes startling ones. The Lord says, "Listen! I am standing at the door, knocking; if you hear my voice and open the door, I will come in to you and eat with you, and you with me" (Rev. 3:20). This form of meditation is a way to fulfill this promise. You may even want to envision opening a door and dining with the Lord. Sometimes within the meditative state a sort of conversation begins to unfold with minimum direction from sense of self. It is as if a lower aspect of being is communicating with a deeper, wiser aspect.

As with anything, the more time spent practicing, the more blessing you will receive in turn. Unlike most disciplines, however, I don't think of meditating as achieving or even learning something. Rather, it seems more like awakening from the blinders and chains of the delusion of self and all the concerns and troubles associated with that delusion. Once in a state of meditation, many possibilities await. Enjoy the ride.

ABOUT THE COVER PHOTO

E. Kent Rogers is the founder, director, and house father of the New Life
Children's Home, an orphanage in Kathmandu, Nepal. He tells the following
story about the photo on the cover of this book:

The teens of our children's home and I had taken a bumpy, cliff-
clinging, death-defying, vomit-filled, and terrifying bus ride to Lang-
tang National Park, Nepal, for a trek in the Himalayas. All the kids
voted to avoid taking the same bus ride again by walking back to
Kathmandu through the foothills. This meant we had to walk hard
and far each day to make our budget fit and to get back in time for
school.

About five days in, we had what turned out to be one of the most
grueling days of the whole trek. We had taken a "shortcut" that included a lot of unexpected extra ups and downs, scrambling through
brush, and a dangerous walk along a narrow cliff ledge. By afternoon,
we were all spent. But we had to keep going. The last leg of the day's
hike entailed walking straight up the side of a steep slope for an alti-
tude increase of nearly a mile. We finally got to the top of the ridge
and collapsed on a patch of grass. My back was aching. The children
looked sullen, and I couldn't blame them. In fact, I was very impressed
with them, since the only person complaining was me. I wondered
what had possessed me to embark on this madman's journey.

Just then a local girl of about seven came to the edge of the circle of our tattered band and smiled. She asked if we were looking for Chandanbari, a nearby village. I wearily nodded. She said, "It is near," and beckoned us to follow her. She led us along a level path (hallelujah!) and soon we entered a wondrous virgin forest of massive oaks, pines, and blooming rhododendrons. Shafts of light from the setting sun danced between the waves of mist that were rolling up the hill from far below. Above, the branches were draped with Spanish moss, and below, the forest floor was clad with a delicate, pink-flowered shrub that emitted a fragrance that can only be described as celestial.

I suddenly knew why we had embarked on our trek. This was among the most movingly serene and beautiful places I'd ever experienced. I felt as if we were being led into heaven itself by our little angel guide. When we arrived at our destination, we met other trekkers, who were still enthusing about "the enchanted forest." The photo of the front cover is of one corner of the magical, secluded forest described above.

The way to peace and joy often requires us to first tread the painful path of introspection and change. Heaven is sometimes a moment away from our times of deepest despair and pain. Don't give up—an angel is around the corner!